141 - DELIGHTERS &
142 - DELIGHTERS IN
148 - 5 YR EXAMPLE
166 - ALLOCATION FOR GROWTH STAGE
180 - DEVELOP FOR INTERNAL USERS LIKE EXTERNAL
192 - LET THE CUSTOMER SPEAK
198 - IMPORTANCE VS SATISFACTION SURVEY
217 - ONLY COMMUNICATE ROADMAP IF REVENUE
270 - HIGH LEVEL BULLETS

BUILD WHAT MATTERS

68   10X OUTCOME

BUILD
WHAT
MATTERS

DELIVERING KEY OUTCOMES
WITH VISION-LED
PRODUCT MANAGEMENT

BEN FOSTER &
RAJESH NERLIKAR

LIONCREST
PUBLISHING

BUILD WHAT MATTERS
Delivering Key Outcomes with Vision-Led Product Management

ISBN 978-1-5445-1618-9   *Hardcover*
       978-1-5445-1617-2   *Paperback*
       978-1-5445-1619-6   *Ebook*

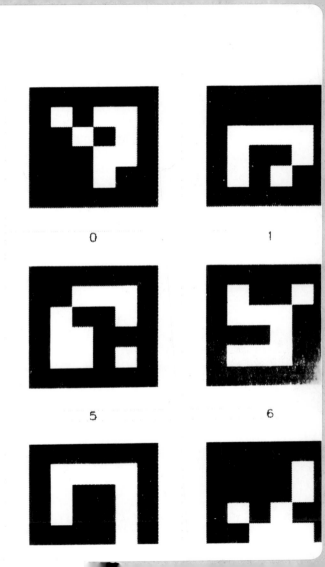

0

1

5

6

CONTENTS

INTRODUCTION

Product management is a paradox. Consider the following questions:

- Does product management deliver outcomes for the business or the customer?
- Is product management an art or a science?
- Does product management succeed by setting the right priorities now or by planning farther ahead?
- Should product managers be held fully accountable for results, or do they lack the necessary authority?

We could keep going with these kinds of questions, but the answer to all of them would still be the same: both! That's the inherent complexity of product management. It's the reason so many companies struggle to understand the role, and even the companies who "totally get it" end up struggling anyway. The paradox of product management is also what makes it so fascinating, and in many ways, it's why we wrote this book. Guiding success in product management and product leadership, in particular, is the challenge that this book aims to address.

In our work as product management advisors, we've spoken to leaders of more than 250 organizations and spent thousands of hours with clients, advising and coaching more than sixty SaaS, enterprise, and consumer tech companies. What has become clear to us through our experience is that product management is hard. It is also one of the most important functions in tech companies, so despite its difficulty, it's critical to get it right.

We've seen some hard-working product teams crash and burn, taking their companies down with them, and we've seen other hard-working product teams thrive, leading their companies to phenomenal growth. What makes the difference?

As it turns out, effective product teams have one thing in common: a consistent **focus on the customer** that allows them to paint a clear picture of the **product vision** for helping customers achieve **key outcomes,** which are necessary to **achieve business goals.** This book is intended to show founders, product leaders, aspiring product leaders, and investors who are seeking to maximize results how to create that consistent customer focus and product vision.

We've observed a common theme of companies overemphasizing minor optimizations, which distract attention from the more important question of how to better deliver value to current and future customers in the long run. Without a clear vision of the end-state that they are working toward, the ensuing debates and discussions result in suboptimal outcomes at best, and at worst, can become death spirals for the product or even the whole company.

Consider your own experiences in product management. If you're a product manager or leader, do you repeatedly struggle to make decisions about what should go in the next sprint? Do you feel like you lack a clear sense of direction for product development? Do you get hit from all sides by people with competing ideas or opposing objectives? If you're a founder, CEO, or investor, have you observed these struggles on your product team?

Product managers have to deal with a heavy volume of feedback: customers criticizing the product and demanding additional features, engineers bemoaning outdated infrastructure or technical debt, and internal stakeholders with misaligned expectations. Pleasing everyone can be challenging and exhausting, and a lack of direction forces many product managers to make poor decisions. As a result, many product managers find themselves on the defensive, operating as gatekeepers against inbound requests. They react to outside pressure instead of setting an end goal for their product and moving tenaciously toward it.

We believe the best defense is a good offense. To go on the offensive, you must get a step ahead of the inbound requests and set a concrete vision for your product that is grounded in customer research, and build buy-in across the organization for strategic milestones to achieve that vision. That's the core of the *Vision-Led Product Management* framework, which we will cover in detail in this book.

WHO WE ARE

We are Ben Foster and Rajesh Nerlikar, and we would like to share our stories, so you understand why we are so passionate about product management.

Ben's Story

I graduated from UC Berkeley at the pinnacle of the internet revolution. Being in Silicon Valley at that time was an incredible way to start my career. A few years in, when the dot-com bubble burst, most companies were downsizing or going bankrupt, but one big company was still hiring like crazy: eBay.

eBay was growing at an impressive rate due in large part to the leadership of its senior VP of product, legendary tech product mastermind Marty Cagan. In many ways, Marty laid the foundation for modern-day product management: empowering product managers and focusing on results over delivery. Being a product manager there was like being on a dynastic college basketball team with a championship-winning coach. The product improvements I helped deliver yielded more than a dozen patents and drove over $100 million to the bottom line. My years at eBay were a whirlwind experience, and I learned many of the fundamentals I still rely on to this day.

In 2010, I moved to the East Coast and joined an energy-efficiency startup in Arlington, VA called Opower, where I met a talented product manager named Rajesh Nerlikar. As VP of product at Opower, I brought my Silicon Valley leadership experience to the company and, more broadly, to the D.C. region. During my tenure, Opower grew from an early-stage startup to a successful growth-stage SaaS company and then to a thriving publicly traded company valued at over $1 billion.

Wanting to share what I'd learned with the leaders of other companies, I spent the next four years as a product advisor for more than forty tech companies, laying the groundwork for what would eventually become the product management advisory firm Prodify. Through my time at these companies, I observed similarities among successful product teams. The ones that achieved amazing outcomes tended to connect their own business success back to customer outcomes, while those that struggled seemed to exhibit a wide range of unhealthy patterns.

Seeking to apply the frameworks I had established in my advisory positions, I returned to operating roles, first as chief product officer of the SaaS company GoCanvas, then at the consumer wearable company WHOOP, where I am currently chief product officer.

Rajesh's Story

I cut my teeth as a software engineer and startup founder before stepping into my first official role as a product manager on Ben's team at Opower. While there, I learned the foundations of customer-centric product management. I went on to become senior product manager at HelloWallet and then Director of Workplace Products for Morningstar, where I managed a $40 million product portfolio with a team of twenty people, which included product managers, technical project managers, and product operations/support. I'm now serving as the VP of product at Savonix, a Prodify client and healthcare startup in the Bay Area focused on fighting dementia.

My journey to product advisor and coach started at the Chicago tech and entrepreneurship accelerator 1871, where I enjoyed sharing the product lessons I'd learned with early-stage startups and found myself learning a lot in doing so. When I moved to Austin, I reached out to Ben, and we started working together again, helping other product teams succeed. Eventually, he became CPO at GoCanvas, and I took over the advisory work and operations at Prodify.

WHY WE WROTE THIS BOOK

Through our experiences, we've seen numerous examples of amazing product management, but we've also seen far too many companies limping along with unclear decision-making and muddled ideas. Some great products and promising startups have circled the drain when they should have been building what matters. Through our advisory work at Prodify, we're aiming to make a difference for tech companies with untapped potential, so we created the Vision-Led Product Management framework and wrote this book to codify all of the best practices we've shared with clients in a way that would be both understandable and actionable.

In the following pages, you won't encounter random musings on product management or career advice for product managers. Instead, we aim to provide expert guidance to strengthen your product leadership mindset and maximize the impact of your product development efforts.

We'll share best practices for putting together an effective team aligned with your vision and implementing repeatable processes to achieve it. You'll also learn how to conduct customer research and make it a habit for your product team. After all, a great product vision can't be based on guesswork alone, nor can you create it solely within the four walls of your office or over Zoom.

In each chapter, we have included stories from our own successes and failures in product management. Along with our own stories, we will share client case studies so you can see these concepts in action. While we will refer to a few well-known product examples from established companies like Amazon and Tesla, our focus throughout the book is on real-world tech companies that look much like your own. Through these firsthand accounts and client case studies, we will help you understand the *application* of key points in the book.

In the end, we hope to give you confidence in determining the *how* and *why* of your product development efforts, so you can drive better outcomes for your customers and your business. As you develop an increasingly coherent end-state vision for your product and the ability to communicate a strong rationale for your development priorities, you will strengthen your position as a product leader.

PART

I

MAKING PRODUCT MANAGEMENT WORK

CHAPTER ONE

WHY PRODUCT ISN'T WORKING

"Happy families are all alike; every unhappy family is unhappy in its own way."
—Leo Tolstoy, *Anna Karenina*

We see hard-working product teams struggling all the time, even under the best of conditions. While there are many things that can go wrong, we've identified the most common dysfunctions in product management. If some of these seem familiar, then this is the book for you.

TOP TEN DYSFUNCTIONS IN PRODUCT MANAGEMENT

Here are the top ten dysfunctions in product management from our perspective:

TOP 10 DYSFUNCTIONS OF PRODUCT MANAGEMENT

1. THE HAMSTER WHEEL
A focus on output over outcomes.

2. THE COUNTING HOUSE
An obsession with internal metrics.

3. THE IVORY TOWER
A lack of customer research.

4. THE SCIENCE LAB
Optimization to the exclusion of all else.

5. THE FEATURE FACTORY
An assembly line of features.

6. THE BUSINESS SCHOOL
The overuse of science and data.

7. THE ROLLER COASTER
Fast-paced twists and turns.

8. THE BRIDGE TO NOWHERE
Overengineering for future unknowns.

9. THE NEGOTIATING TABLE
Trying to keep everyone happy.

10. THE THRONE ROOM
Whipsaw decision-making from the person in charge.

We'll delve into each of these dysfunctions so you can see if they are representative of the challenges you're dealing with in your company. You may find you've experienced most or even *all* of them at one time or another. Rest assured that doesn't signal incompetence or imply your product team is deficient or unskilled. On the contrary, these issues are so prevalent that almost everyone who has worked in product management will have struggled with them at one point or another. As you read each of them, mark which ones ring true at your company.

Pattern #1: The Hamster Wheel

On a hamster wheel, all that matters is continuing to run, even though you're not getting anywhere. Similarly, we find that sometimes product teams are almost entirely focused on hitting deadlines with little regard for the outcome. When desired outcomes are unclear or difficult to measure, leadership tends to concentrate on *output* instead, but what's the use of spending months developing a product that no customer wants or is willing to pay for, whether you hit the deadline or not?

If you're delivering the wrong thing, it doesn't matter how efficiently or quickly you deliver it, and your output isn't necessarily meaningful or beneficial unless you're creating value for the customer or the business.

Compare these two questions, and you'll see the difference in perspective.

- Did you ship that feature on time? (output-oriented)
- Did that feature deliver value to customers and grow revenue? (outcome-oriented)

Ben's Story

MEASURING LINES OF PRD

During my time at eBay, from 2001 to 2005, product management was run by a few different leaders. When I first joined as an entry-level product manager, Marty Cagan was leading product management and design, and there was a true appreciation for the innovative role that product management played. After he left, the engineering leader stepped in to fill his shoes. Her perspective was that product management's job was to feed the engineering beast, producing volumes of product requirements documents (PRDs) that would keep thousands of developers busy. The joint product and engineering team became extremely efficient at delivering lots of *code*, less so at delivering consistent *results*.

With no clear way of holding product managers accountable for outcomes, she defaulted to pure productivity metrics. Product managers were actually issued a quota for *lines of PRD written per quarter,* and that quota was increased each quarter to demonstrate productivity gains to the COO.

The consequences were predictable. Product managers worked excessively long hours to produce monster PRDs for overdesigned features. I personally wrote a 240-page PRD that required an entire week of meetings to hand off to the engineering team. Looking back, I'm confident the same results could have been delivered with a simplified product design and less documentation, which would have saved engineering

capacity and allowed us to address the next business opportunity. Believe it or not, at the time, I was actually *proud of
myself*. In what should have been a "teaching moment," I was
applauded for the time I put in and the amount of work I created for others.

Pattern #2: The Counting House

In the counting house, the focus is entirely on internal metrics with no regard for customer success. Many product
teams become obsessed with internal metrics like revenue
growth, monthly active users (MAUs), and customer retention.
Sometimes, they even fabricate new metrics because they're
convinced that if some internal number looks good, it must
mean the product is a success.

The truth is, most internal metrics are *trailing* indicators of
a product's success, and therefore shouldn't be the primary
focus of product management. It's far better to answer the
question, "How can we effectively deliver greater value to our
customers?" If you can answer that question and create a good
business model around the answer, your internal metrics will
almost always follow suit.

Pattern #3: The Ivory Tower

In the ivory tower, product teams become so removed, so
far *above* the customers that they start thinking they know
their customers better than the customers know themselves.
Consequently, they never really talk to their customers, which

means they risk building a product no one wants or needs. Just because a product team falls in love with its own solution doesn't mean customers will.

Furthermore, a lack of customer-driven insights can lead to a spiral of mistrust between product management and other stakeholder groups in the company. Product management feels like they are building the right product (though they may not be), so when the product doesn't perform well in the market, they assume the fault lies elsewhere. Go-to-market teams believe product management is to blame for not being responsive enough to their feedback. Engineering loses confidence that their efforts are worthwhile, and they question every new priority that's presented. From the CEO's perspective, it's unclear why the budget allocated to research and development (R&D) isn't delivering results, and every attempt to figure it out yields more finger-pointing and excuses.

Rajesh's Story
ASSUMING WHAT USERS WANT

Spring 2014 was an exciting time for me. Not only was our first son due, but I also saw two exits from the startups I worked for. Opower went public in April, and HelloWallet was acquired by a strategic investor, Morningstar, in May. Nervous about working for a "big" enterprise like Morningstar, I immediately decided to launch a dating app my buddy and I had been talking about for years. The idea was simple: matching people based on the *actual* places they go because people are more likely to be interested in someone who goes to the same bars, restaurants, parks, museums, and ballparks. Location-based check-ins on Facebook and Foursquare (Swarm) were rising, so we pulled data from those platforms. I called the app Wentroductions, and to this day, I cringe at the awkward name choice.

While deciding on the scope of the minimum viable product (MVP), I used dating app feedback from my friends and my own experiences, but I didn't conduct enough customer discovery to validate our experiences or to understand why someone would use our product over more popular apps like Tinder. Instead, I spent my nights and weekends writing user stories and putting together wireframes so my cousin's software development firm in India could build the MVP. My buddy and I formed a company and put in our own money (I decided to "let it ride" with my two recent exit earnings). About five months later, the app was nearly ready, and I started running Twitter ads to get users.

And then I realized my mistake. We had ten to twelve users in the first two weeks, but dating apps don't succeed if they can't match you with someone soon after you sign up. So I asked friends and family to join because I didn't want to use the common "seed and weed" strategy of creating fake profiles and then removing them when enough users sign up.

I probably don't have to tell you how this ended. Wentroductions never took off with users, and while the app looked and worked great, the product failed as I sat in my ivory tower. It had been *years* since I'd last used a dating app, yet I still thought I knew what users wanted. To this day, my best piece of advice to anyone who thinks a new product should exist in the world is to build a simple landing page and create an email waitlist based on a few simple feature descriptions to learn what resonates with *real customers.*

Pattern #4: The Science Lab

In the science lab, product teams tend to focus all of their efforts on highly measurable yet superficial improvements to their product. Collectively, these small-scale A/B tests don't do much to innovate or add customer value.

Here's a version of this problem we often see. A company has a sign-up process on their website, and they want to encourage more people to use it. To do that, they start making a variety of minor optimizations to the sign-up process—changing button colors, tweaking the text, changing the graphics—hoping that *something* will drive up the level of engagement. In general, these kinds of changes provide no actual value to customers and have very little to do with engagement.

In the last few years, we've seen optimization become the be-all and end-all for more and more companies rather than a facet of a balanced product development roadmap. The assumption is that making improvements to existing solutions is the one thing that will drive results, but even effective optimizations can't take the place of real innovation. Companies that are constantly trying to eke out more value from their existing solutions run the risk of stagnating. It's almost impossible to A/B test your way to real innovation.

Pattern #5: The Feature Factory

What does a feature factory build? Features. When is a feature factory done building features? Never. The problem with being a feature factory is that there's always the next one to build. Product teams fall into this trap because they are led to believe by customers or internal stakeholders that if they just had *this one next feature*, they will close incremental deals or keep customers who might otherwise leave.

Sometimes, it works out that a specific missing feature is holding the business back, but more often than not, the team discovers that yet another feature is also needed. Even when the newest addition does, in fact, fully resolve a customer's issue such that it saves an account or lands a new deal, it's only one. All the while, *entire market opportunities* are missed because the product doesn't deliver sufficient value to prospective customers who lack a voice (or won't bother speaking). In fact, the addition of too many features can weigh down the user experience (UX) so much that new customers can no longer comprehend the product, which results in a net negative outcome for the company.

Ben's Story
THE COLOR-CODED ROADMAP

I vividly remember joining Opower as the VP of product in early 2010. In my second week, the board requested to see a product roadmap. Scrambling to deliver, the obvious starting point was learning from the team what had already been planned. In doing so, I discovered two surprising facts: 1) there was no roadmap, and 2) the company had already contractually committed nearly all of the engineering capacity for the next six months to building a hodgepodge of one-off features for newly-closed accounts.

These weren't the priorities I wanted, and in fact, no one else in the company wanted them prioritized either, but in an effort to close business, they had acquiesced. I needed to communicate to the board and our employees not only what our priorities were but why, so I created a roadmap document that showed all of the features we were required to build over the next six months color-coded in yellow and all the more meaningful improvements we were excited to deliver afterward color-coded in blue. That way everyone saw the reality but also had a glimmer of hope: after heads-down work for six months, we would be in a position to really innovate.

Sadly, that's not what happened. Six months later, we had indeed delivered against the client commitments, but the color-coded roadmap still looked exactly the same. In that time, we had continued to make new client commitments, deferring our intended priorities another six months. This would have continued into perpetuity if we hadn't solved the underlying problem. We were a feature factory! With some great cross-functional teamwork, we were finally able to break away from this pattern. Later in the book, we'll discuss the resolution and finish this story.

Pattern #6: The Business School

Business school is where you go to *analyze* business but not to actually *do* business. Similarly, product teams can get so wrapped up in overanalyzing everything that they avoid making tough but essential judgment calls. When it comes to prioritization, some product managers are tempted to get so technical and mathematical that they lose perspective.

There's a process that seems to make sense to product teams. They sit down and draw up a list of all the features and improvements they want to make to their product. Then they work with the finance team to generate estimates about the specific business impact of these features. Finally, they meet with the engineering team to figure out how much effort it's going to take to develop them.

Having done that, they typically conduct net present value (NPV) or return on investment (ROI) analyses for every feature or improvement, do scenario-planning, and create spreadsheets that reveal the estimated monetary impact of each potential feature divided by the amount of effort it will take to develop. Whatever winds up with the biggest number gets top priority, and they declare, "The mathematics have spoken! Our product decisions have revealed themselves!"

It sounds great in theory, but in reality, no product *decisions* are being made at all. The initiatives that show the highest estimated impact are the ones that were modeled using the most outrageous assumptions, and usually only the lowest-effort improvements end up above the cutline. All the while, customers and the larger business strategy are completely ignored. Arming oneself with specious ROI estimates at a committee meeting is a poor substitute for making the right strategic decisions to maximize the impact of product development.

Pattern #7: The Roller Coaster

A roller coaster is all about fast thrills and wild, whiplashing movements. They can be a lot of fun, but they aren't a good model for effective product management. Investors and executives like to see immediate results, and when those results don't materialize right away, they can be tempted to pivot suddenly, resulting in whiplash for the product team.

This problem comes from setting a time horizon that is too short. For startups, a lack of patience is often the result of having a very short runway. They have to get something up and running fast so they can raise the next round of funding, or they need to start producing revenue right away.

Of course, everyone wants to make fast and efficient progress, but providing insufficient opportunity for success will result in false negatives that can lead product managers astray. When an otherwise healthy "fail-fast" mentality is taken *to the extreme*, it can stifle innovation.

"We think this new feature is a good idea," a product manager might say. "To avoid overinvesting, we'll first launch a lackluster version of it. If it doesn't get overwhelmingly positive results immediately, then we'll know it's not the right direction for our product." Daisy-chained together, these false negatives result in a headache-inducing roller coaster ride for product development that ends up in exactly the same place it started.

Pattern #8: The Bridge to Nowhere

Engineers love solving future problems with technology. That can be a good thing when taken to the right level, but it can also be taken too far. They get excited about developing the infrastructure to get the product *just right*, but sometimes, they can end up *overengineering* a product, trying to account for future needs that aren't relevant—and may never be. As a result, product development can get so bogged down that a great product that would have delivered meaningful customer value never sees the light of day.

Sometimes, it's better for engineers to tolerate some reworking of the product down the road, as long as the foundational elements are in place, rather than solving numerous theoretical and potential problems. Imagine if a team of engineers designed and constructed a bridge over a river to connect a city to a wilderness area where another city *might* someday exist. They invest a tremendous amount of time, money, and resources to construct a bridge sturdy enough to support a multilane highway under the assumption that eventually there will be a lot of traffic, but what would be the point if the second city never got built? Why not wait until at least a small town has developed on the other side of the river, and then build a small, one-lane bridge to connect it, with the understanding that if the town grows into a large city, the bridge can be expanded and reinforced?

Every tech company has to invest in the underlying technology of its product, but there must be sufficient confidence that it will offer tangible value to the business or the customer within a reasonable time frame to warrant investment now. Scaling for a future that never materializes is a futile exercise no tech company can afford.

Pattern #9: The Negotiating Table

Sometimes, product meetings can turn into a negotiating table, as the product manager tries to give everyone what they want. Product managers often believe that success means keeping all of their stakeholders happy—or, at least, minimizing their unhappiness—but when teams and individuals throughout the organization collectively want more than engineering can potentially deliver, this becomes practically impossible. A list of inbound demands might look like this:

- The CEO has a pet product idea.
- Sales wants five other features.
- Engineering feels it's critical to tackle some technical debt.
- Customer support needs a bug fix.

How can the product manager satisfy all of these requests in a timely manner, so they get that all-important pat on the back from everyone?

It's a bit like playing a game of high-stakes Tetris, as product managers try to fit all of the incongruent requests together. In a sense, they wind up prioritizing to avoid discomfort with the people they see every day in the office. Of course, nobody wants their colleagues mad at them.

However, it's not a leader's job to give everyone what they want, and, in fact, true leadership requires making some unpopular decisions. Product teams find themselves in the negotiating table situation when the organization misunderstands product management's chief purpose. It's not the primary role of product management to help sales hit their quota this quarter. It's the role of product management to make it possible for sales to sign up for higher quotas than anyone thought possible farther in the future. When product management prioritizes the right things for the customer, they help *every* team, whether those teams realize it or not.

Pattern #10: The Throne Room

Sometimes, the founder or CEO just can't let go. They feel compelled to make decisions about anything and everything important in the company, and they give their team very little ability to call their own shots. Because their instincts got them to where they are, they think it will continue to carry them forward, but at a certain point, instinct doesn't scale. Their job title becomes a trump card any time they want to override a creative decision, and they might not even bother to clarify the rationale when they throw their weight around.

They fail to drive alignment around the product direction, so no one really understands what they're doing or why. In these kinds of situations, the CEO typically changes their mind frequently, sometimes with little notice, and usually with no real explanation or justification. Every request is treated as priority number one, and the product manager is expected to give them 100 percent of their attention.

It's an impossible situation for a product team that prevents the scaling of the company beyond a single decision-maker. There must be a clear framework around prioritization that everyone in the company understands, so every initiative can be properly evaluated to determine if it contributes to the end-state customer vision and ultimate success of the company.

Ben's Story
CONSTANTLY CHANGING PRIORITIES

When I joined Adchemy, a twenty-five-person startup, in 2006 the company had already built ingenious machine learning technology capable of generating and optimizing billions of ads and landing pages every day. The promise of that technology led to multiple funding rounds and a $400 million valuation in 2009.

The difficulty was in converting that technology into a viable product in the competitive ad tech space. Do you sell it to publishers? To advertisers? To agencies? Should it be applied to paid search or display ads or landing pages? Do you package the technology or use it yourself to outperform other affiliate partners delivering online leads? As I moved up the ranks to eventually lead product management and design at Adchemy, I needed clarity, or at least agreement, from the co-founder/CEO on which of these paths we should choose.

The CEO was exceptionally good at setting a single priority and aligning everyone to it. The only problem was that the singular priority changed like clockwork every quarter. Rather than committing to a path, he vented frustrations down the chain about the (unsurprising) lack of progress on the *paths not taken.* My team was forced to shift gears frequently, and with very little rationale offered for the hard pivots he demanded, rallying the troops proved an impossible task. Seeing the writing on the wall, I eventually left and the company was ultimately sold to Walmart Labs with no return for investors.

SCORECARD

As you've read through these ten dysfunctions of product management, at least a few have probably hit close to home. It can be a useful exercise to assess your organization against each one, so we've created this table to help you do just that. Give yourself a point for each problem that you are struggling with in your company, then add up the total and see where things stand.

Ten Dysfunctions of Product Management: Self-Assessment

- ☐ The Hamster Wheel: output over outcomes
- ☐ The Counting House: obsession with internal metrics
- ☐ The Ivory Tower: lack of customer research
- ☐ The Science Lab: optimization to the exclusion of everything else
- ☐ The Feature Factory: an assembly line of features
- ☐ The Business School: overdependence on data and spreadsheets
- ☐ The Roller Coaster: fast-paced twists and turns
- ☐ The Bridge to Nowhere: overengineering for future unknowns
- ☐ The Negotiating Table: trying to keep everyone happy

☐ The Throne Room: whipsaw decision-making from the person in charge

SCORING

0 points: Wow! Maybe *you* should write a book on product management.

1 point: Amazing! You'd be valedictorian of your product class.

2 points: Not bad. You're keeping up with other product teams.

3 points: Hmm. You've got some work to do.

4+ points: Oof! You've got your work cut out for you. Take detailed notes as you read this book and make specific plans for how you'll fix these dysfunctions at your company.

Think about the impact it would make if you resolved all of those dysfunctions in your organization. Consider all of the engineering potential and creative energy it would free up. Now, consider the unmeasured cost of *not* dealing with them. Your engineers are probably some of your highest paid, highest value employees, so if their effort isn't aligned to the right activities, it's probably costing you more than you realize.

THE COMMONALITIES

While these dysfunctions may seem like ten completely different problems, they fall under just three basic themes:

1. Internal focus is drawing too much attention away from delivering meaningful customer value.

2. The product team is so busy playing defense or has so little authority, there is no time left for ideation and innovation.

3. The desire for short-term directly measurable business outcomes results in only superficial changes being prioritized.

In essence, these themes are all ways that a company naturally fills gaps that could be filled with a clear direction and path for the product. When we spoke with Gibson Biddle, former VP of product management at Netflix and highly regarded product management thought leader, he explained this succinctly: "Product leadership is defined as inspired communication of a vision. The majority of problems faced by most product teams are solved through strong leadership."

Creating an end-state customer vision for your product is how to resolve each of these ten patterns of dysfunction, both by uprooting them and by preventing them from taking hold in the first place. It also prevents product manager burnout. These problems exact a heavy toll, and when they mount up, even a hardened product manager can become so worn out and discouraged that they quit. We've seen this happen firsthand, so we always love it when we can help a product manager overcome these challenges and ease the burden.

ACTION CHECKLIST AND RESOURCES

We want this book to be actionable and helpful to everyone who reads it, so at the end of each chapter, we've included a link to an action checklist and resources that will make it easy to take those actions. That way, you can apply the concepts from each chapter to your own product(s).

Visit *buildwhatmattersbook.com* for an action checklist and additional resources, such as a team-level scorecard for the ten dysfunctions in your organization.

CHAPTER 2

THE SOLUTION

"The best defense is a good offense."
—Pretty Much Every Strategist Ever

When you look at the problems from the previous chapter, it's easy to see why so many product teams are overwhelmed, frustrated, or confused. In this chapter, we will reveal a framework for resolving those top ten dysfunctions, and then, throughout the rest of the book, we will delve into the actual process for creating your vision and putting together the right team and processes to implement it effectively. In the end, we're confident it will be transformative for your product management practice.

It all starts with becoming truly product-driven.

BEING PRODUCT-DRIVEN

Most of the founders, CEOs, and product managers we speak to either claim that their companies are product-driven or say,

"We're not there yet, but we certainly aspire to be." However, when we start probing for specifics—*What does it mean to be product-driven? How do you know you're moving in that direction? How will you know when you've achieved it?* —more often than not, we get blank stares in return.

This is indicative of a larger problem across the entire spectrum of the tech and startup world. Company leaders want to be product-driven, but they don't know what being "product-driven" (or "product-led") means exactly. There are two core operating tenets of being a product-driven company:

1. You address a customer's need through a solution applicable to the broader market.
2. Product decisions come first, and other decisions follow.

Let's unpack each of these.

A Solution for a Broader Market

The first tenet of a product-driven company is that it builds solutions that work for an entire market segment, rather than for one customer at a time. In any given market, each potential customer will have their own individual needs, preferences, priorities, and trade-offs they are willing to make.

Imagine you could make a map of all the potential customers in your market and their respective desires for a solution and plot them as dots. Some customers would have very similar desires, and other customers' opposing preferences would place them far away from one another.

Different customers appearing in different areas of the map represent how their ideal solutions are also unique. In order to perfectly satisfy every customer's desires, you would have to deliver a specially tailored solution for each of them, which is exactly what services-driven companies do. Those solutions could be delivered via ongoing services (as a consultancy does) or by delivering bespoke technology solutions, as represented by the squares on the map.

How a Services-Driven Company Delivers Solutions

Every Customer's
Individual Desires

Custom Solution
For Every Customer

Systems integrator Accenture is a quintessential services-driven company. They want to be able to say yes to any request for proposal (RFP) a customer submits. When a potential client comes to them and says, "We need this project done for us," they bend over backward to fulfill that request and capture the revenue. In practice, they end up providing many different one-off custom solutions to keep new and existing customers happy. This is appropriate in certain situations, when each customer's need is highly specific and when the solution needs to work in an *exact* way.

A product-driven company takes the exact opposite approach from a services-driven company. They never build a custom solution for an individual customer. Instead, they build a *product* that they expect multiple customers to adopt once available.

In theory, product-driven companies gamble that the product they've created will address the needs of many customers, including those they haven't yet met. While a services-driven company first needs to meet the customer to understand their individual needs so they can custom-build a solution for them, a product-driven company creates a product based on an educated guess about what the needs of future prospective customers will be. This changes *everything* about the company's operations and places an enormous burden on product management to get it right.

For most prospective customers, the product will be less than perfect in some way. Does that mean the product will only be a viable solution for the narrow range of customers whose ideal desires are met by the product? *No!* Prospective customers who can imagine some product improvement will still buy and be very satisfied with the product. The product doesn't need to be perfect for every customer—it just has to be *the best solution available.*

This is where companies that *aspire to be* product-driven often get it wrong: they ask existing customers what they want the product to do that it doesn't currently do. There will always be a million answers to that question, and sometimes those answers will be in direct conflict with one another. You will never finish building a product that makes every customer in the target market perfectly satisfied. After all, that's the approach of a services-driven company, not a product-driven company. To avoid unintentionally becoming a services-driven company, you must say no to most product requests.

The reason we're providing so much theory about being product-driven is because it's absolutely essential to embrace the reality that there will *always* be gaps between how your target market wants your product to work and how it actually works. This point is so important, it bears repeating:

*Embrace the reality that there will **always** be gaps between what your customer wants and what your product does.*

Those gaps aren't just tolerable, they are necessary. If you were to successfully close all of them, you would either fork the code so much, or you would end up with a product so bloated that it would become unusable due to its complexity. If the gaps between your product capabilities and your customers' desires are small enough that the product is clearly the best option for them, and will likely continue to be for the foreseeable future, then don't get distracted by their requests.

Of course, you are bound to get feedback from customers who are dealing with gaps so wide that they cannot use the product, or they can find a better alternative. The important consideration in this case is whether or not those customers are part of your target market.

None of this is to say that you shouldn't listen to your current customers. However, as a product-driven company, how you *interpret* what your customers tell you matters greatly. If there is a way to address the feedback such that it will benefit other customers and the business as well, then doing so may be worthwhile as it will get you closer to product-market fit (PMF). If what you're building only benefits the customer you're talking to but is unlikely to benefit anyone else, then you're listening to your customers but not being product-driven.

How A Product-Driven Company Delivers Solutions

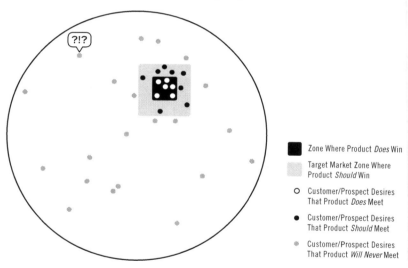

■ Zone Where Product *Does* Win

▨ Target Market Zone Where Product *Should* Win

○ Customer/Prospect Desires That Product *Does* Meet

● Customer/Prospect Desires That Product *Should* Meet

※ Customer/Prospect Desires That Product *Will Never* Meet

Let's look at an updated version of the customer desires map to illustrate how a product-driven company operates.

- The black square is the portion of your target market that your product currently serves well. The white dots are

the customers and prospects for whom your product is a
clear winner.

- The gray box represents your broader target market,
  and the black dots inside of it represent the desires of
  customers and prospects that you aim to serve as you
  improve your product to expand its reach. In order to
  win them over, you need to understand their desires and
  close the gap between what the product does today and
  what they want it to do.
- The gray dots outside of the target market box are the
  desires of customers and prospects for whom the product
  was not designed. *Of course* the product won't work as
  they would like; it was never meant to.

This graphic can also help explain how a product-driven
company interprets feedback from customers and prospects.
A product-driven company has a clearly defined target market
(the gray box) and knows which segments of that target market the product currently serves well (the black box and white
dots). Knowing their product will attract all three types of customers, a product-driven company first determines which type
of customer they're talking to before deciding how to respond
to the feedback.

- If the feedback is coming from someone whose desires
  are met by the current product (a white dot), they need
  to decide whether responding to that feedback is going
  to help the business through retention or upsells.
  If doing so carries no significant business benefits,

then the company may be chasing rainbows by working down a never-ending list of potential product enhancements. While it may be tempting to drive customer satisfaction, customers usually just end up fixating on the next missing feature instead.

- If the feedback comes from someone in the target market (a black dot), the product-driven company will synthesize that feedback to determine how to improve their fit and deepen their market penetration by better addressing a wider range of customer desires.

- If the feedback comes from someone outside of the target market (a gray dot), the product-driven company knows to disregard the feedback, unless they are intentionally expanding their target market to cover that type of customer. You see this as the gray dot in the top left, the customer who bought your product intending to use it for a purpose it was never meant for and who vents frustrations in the form of demands and threats to abandon the product. It's hard to do, but a product-driven company will let them go.

Product Decisions Come First

Think of a company as a series of interoperating gears. Where the gears mesh is how the functional teams work together. With any system of gears, there's one gear that has the drive—the one connected to the motor.

The second core operating tenet of being a product-driven company is that the product is the driver. This means figuring out what the market needs are going to be and constructing a product that will meet them for a broad set of customers. Everybody in the company—sales, marketing, engineering, and so on—rallies around the product strategy. The end-state customer vision provides direction and alignment for the entire team, and product management is responsible for creating that vision and sharing it with all stakeholders.

There are other options besides being product-driven, and depending on the company, those other options may be more appropriate. For example, we would argue that Nike is a *brand-driven* company, at least for its apparel business. It's all about getting the iconic swoosh out there and associating the brand with the aspirations of their target customer: emulating celebrity athletes, embracing the mentality epitomized by their trademarked "Just Do It" slogan, and reveling in a spirit of competition and commitment. The other divisions are obliged to follow suit and execute their pieces of that strategy. It is unlikely that any designer at Nike would create a new product and then try to figure out, after the fact, where to fit "that darned swoosh." A brand-driven strategy isn't a bad strategy—for Nike.

Certain technology-driven companies, such as those creating artificial intelligence (AI) and augmented reality (AR) capabilities, are also different from product-driven companies because the capabilities they create are licensed by customers to experiment with and explore potential uses. In these companies, *technology* is the driver, and the other organizations in the company must follow their lead. On the cutting edge of technology, where a market doesn't exist yet or is very poorly defined, this may very well be the best approach.

However, the most successful tech companies in the world are product-driven. They identify market opportunities and design solutions that directly address broad market needs while providing strong unit economics. Only afterward do they scale massively by investing in underlying technology, crafting smart product positioning, and executing go-to-market tactics that are well-suited to the product and the market. The product drives everything.

Case Study

CROSSLEAD: CONVERGING ON PRODUCT-MARKET FIT

CrossLead is a platform that helps organizations of all sizes plan, manage, and track progress toward achieving important company objectives. It was founded by Navy SEAL David Silverman, co-author of the best seller *Team of Teams*, which details the military's need to become nimbler and more flexible in order to successfully fight Al Qaeda. Many commercial organizations are faced with the challenge of making similar adaptations, but they lack the necessary software tools and frameworks, which CrossLead provides. Nevertheless, the CrossLead team did not see immediate market traction.

Prodify began working with CrossLead at a time when its leadership was having difficult internal conversations about how to reach product-market fit (PMF). We facilitated an exercise that helped them identify the right path.

As CrossLead's head of product, Paige Morschauser describes the process, "People tend to look at PMF as just 'product' and 'market,' but that is an incomplete way of looking at it. It is important to factor economics into the equation and then consider the intersections between all three areas. Prodify provided us with a Venn diagram of these components and the key success indicators within each. We then individually graded ourselves on each metric before reconvening as a group.

"We used this exercise to facilitate a discussion amongst key stakeholders and to align on the biggest gap within the Venn diagram. For us, it became apparent that there was a disconnect between the value proposition customers looked for during the sales process and what the product delivered after it was purchased."

This insight redirected the company's customer discovery priorities. Next, we worked with Paige's team to develop a new customer research plan to gather further insights from their customers' perspective. The findings led to CrossLead's big "aha" moment, which was that the target buyer persona had been defined so broadly that they could never build enough features to satisfy all of their needs. Debates about which features to put on the roadmap next were the result of there simply being no right answer. They zeroed in on a more specific buyer persona and identified the specific unmet needs that CrossLead should address—all achievable with focused product development efforts.

According to Paige, "We were able to construct a more strategic roadmap spanning the next several quarters and establish important product development milestones that the whole company could rally behind."

HOW TO KNOW WHETHER YOU'RE PRODUCT-DRIVEN

Let's translate the theory into practical terms. How do you know if you are operating as a product-driven company? There are five traits that we see in every product-driven company, so they serve as a good way to determine whether or not your company is there yet.

1. In a product-driven company, product management and user experience (UX) design are the closest parties to the customer. They have an obligation to the rest of the organization to have the best understanding of current and future customers they are designing for, and they build that understanding through frequent interactions with users and through working closely with the customer-facing teams internally.

2. A product-driven company addresses the needs of multiple customers with a single solution (or a handful of solutions) that works for all of them and therefore spends most of its product roadmap on changes that will benefit *many* customers, not just one or two.

Contrast this approach with a services-driven company like Accenture, which develops tailor-made solutions for individual customers.

3. A product-driven company prioritizes the use of technology to solve problems and scale every part of their business. Sometimes, they will initially solve problems manually, but only temporarily—to accelerate time-to-market or reduce risk—as a stopgap until more automated and scalable solutions can be built.

4. A product-driven company listens to current customers and prospects to understand the shifts in market demand and predict the needs of future customers. As in the diagram we referenced previously, this means the product team understands which direction the dots are moving and why and is planning to adapt the product to meet changing desires.

5. While a sales- or services-driven company succeeds by saying *yes* to a specific customer, a product-driven company often succeeds by saying *no*. They recognize that there is a massive opportunity cost in having engineers spend time trying to develop bespoke solutions, which takes critical time and resources away from putting the right product on the shelf to meet future customer needs. The best and most innovative product companies don't have a problem saying no, and they say it often. As Steve Jobs famously put it, "Innovation is saying no to a thousand things."

Case Study

CONTACTUALLY:
THE POWER OF FOCUS

Initially, Contactually was a customer relationship management (CRM) tool for the long tail, allowing small businesses in virtually any industry to manage customer relationships and communications with easy-to-understand, web-based software. The product team had been receiving input from all directions. Customers requested additional features, sales wanted new demo capabilities, customer support identified bugs to fix, and engineering felt an urgency in addressing overdue technical debt. Internal stakeholders became disconnected and frustrated with the product team, yet further trade-offs still needed to be made.

At the same time, co-founders Zvi Band and Tony Cappaert had discovered that they were seeing better traction with real estate agents than customers in other industries, so they were faced with a difficult decision: continue to serve a broad but disjointed customer base or narrow the target market to focus exclusively on the real estate market and risk alienating a subset of (paying) customers.

The company made the difficult but ultimately correct decision to focus its product strategy solely on real estate. As expected, several non-real estate customers failed to renew and new customer acquisition dropped as the product became less relevant to the wider market of small businesses and consultants, but the senior leadership of Contactually understood this was the short-term fallout which would soon be followed by several major benefits.

The marketing and sales teams consolidated go-to-market activities and concentrated messaging on a specific persona. The product management team was able to filter out all inbound requests that weren't directly tied to the needs of real estate agents. They filled the space in the roadmap with items that drove customer value, such as:

- Understanding and solving the more cohesive set of business problems that mattered most to real estate customers.
- Launching real estate-focused onboarding and configurations that improved time to value and utility for end-users and increased average sales price (ASP) by over 50 percent.
- Making a strategic bet to move upmarket to support larger brokerages that contracted with real estate agents.

Rather than building a mediocre product for a broader potential market, Contactually developed a higher quality product for a smaller but still large, accessible market. The results were clear: increases in revenue per customer, willingness to pay, and customer retention. Improvements in growth rate and unit economics eventually led to Contactually's successful exit, as they were acquired by technology-enabled real estate juggernaut Compass.

On reflection, Tony said, "I've become such a big believer in the power of focus. Learning to say 'no' is crucial to success. In doing so, you'll lose some customers, and *that's okay.*"

Zvi added, "Once we focused on real estate, we could concentrate on the cohesive set of user needs and how those translated into larger brokerages as the buyer and user diverged." Both agreed, "Our only regret is that we didn't make these decisions earlier."

WHY BEING
PRODUCT-DRIVEN MATTERS

Why take the gamble to be product-driven? Why not just build according to the specifications of each individual customer, so you never waste time building something nobody is willing to buy? It's because the potential payoff is massive, both to your customers and to your shareholders.

Why It Matters to Your Customers

Let's start by taking a look at what being product-driven does *for your customers.*

First, it helps keep your prices low, and we know a key consideration for customers is price. The cost of delivering a product that has already been built, especially for software, is close to zero, which allows product-driven companies to reduce their prices so much that services-driven companies simply can't compete. Consider the price difference between TurboTax and H&R Block.

Second, it keeps time-to-value low. Having a solution custom-built takes a long time, but pre-built solutions are available immediately—or, at least, deployment can begin immediately—which again puts services-driven companies at a severe disadvantage. Consider how much longer it would take to have custom furniture made versus grabbing a box from IKEA.

Finally, it offers customers the latest-and-greatest. Cloud-based SaaS platforms offer a major advantage in that upgrades can be made once and propagated to all customers either for free or for a modest price increase. In the services-driven model, the fact that each customer has their own solution means each customer needs to pay for one-off improvements to that solution. The high costs of those changes can make the ROI prohibitively low, eventually resulting in an antiquated or obsolete solution. Consider the complexity involved in upgrading decades-old software systems built specifically for the government.

Why It Matters to Your Company

Being product-driven can also have an enormous impact on your company's long-term financial success.

First, being product-driven is more profitable because you've already built the right product for the next customer. The marginal cost of delivering the same repeatable solution to your next customer as you did for your previous customers is extremely low, which improves unit economics and increases the profitability of every sale.

Second, the valuation of a product-driven company is much higher than that of a services-driven company, with six to eight times higher valuations. Sometimes, the fastest path to higher valuation for a services-driven company isn't to grow revenue but to transition their services revenue to product revenue. Some product companies with add-on services go so far as to intentionally partner with services companies to keep the lower gross margin (GM) services revenue off their books.

This difference in revenue multiples is due to higher profitability, scalability, and opportunities for product-led growth that come from being product-driven, creating higher expectations among investors, who will value your current revenue higher as a result. Eric Paley, Managing Partner at Founder Collective—and #9 on the *Forbes* "Midas List" in 2020—explained to us just how important being product-driven is from the investor perspective: "We invest at the seed stage, so the companies we back are still finding their way to product-market fit and massive traction. We have had to get very good at identifying the *precursors* of success, and one of the most important characteristics of a great early-stage investment opportunity is a product orientation from the founding team. Our most successful portfolio companies are the ones that lead with product, meaning they have a well-formed sense of the target market, how those customers are underserved, the drivers of customer value, and how to address the opportunity with a transformative product."

Third, product-driven companies have the unique opportunity to employ product-led growth strategies, such as viral adoption and freemium offerings. Consider a product-driven company like Miro. Miro's product is a collaborative white-board that allows teams to work together remotely, posting ideas, comments, and feedback on a shared space that the entire team can access. With more people working from home following the 2020 coronavirus outbreak, the product has become more popular than ever, and the nature of the product promotes itself. When one person at a company decides to try it, they send invitations to their coworkers. Upon clicking the invitation, those coworkers can access the shared whiteboard and immediately see the power of the product without having to sign up for it, which is an effective way of getting them to discover the value of the product without paying a single advertising dollar or sales commission check. While creating a product-led growth engine like this may be more challenging for some companies than others, it's only feasible for product-driven companies.

INTRODUCING VISION-LED PRODUCT MANAGEMENT

Becoming product-driven is critical for tech companies with big ambitions, and we believe the path to becoming product-driven is to establish a long-term product vision that will meet the needs of your current and future customers.

When we talk about clarifying an end-state vision for your customer, we mean creating a vision for what the future should look like when your product is meeting that new customer's need—*from the customer's perspective*. The vision is not a bulleted list of product features but rather an expression of how the customer will derive value from those features.

VISION-LED PRODUCT MANAGEMENT OVERVIEW

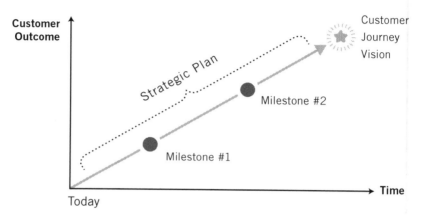

The three core components of the Vision-Led Product Management framework, which we will address in **Part Two** of this book, are key customer outcomes (chapter three), customer journey vision (chapter four), and strategic plan (chapter five).

Key Customer Outcome

In this stage, you determine the right customer outcome to focus on, knowing that if you deliver on an outcome your customers care about, your business success will follow. Once you identify the key customer outcome, you can break it down into specific areas of value creation and strategize accordingly. This is your "metric of progress" to know if the product is delivering value to customers. You will go through a similar exercise to identify the key outcome and contributing factors for your business.

Customer Journey Vision

Your customer journey vision is a description of all aspects of the journey a customer will take with your product to achieve their outcomes, from the initial trigger and discovery, where they become aware of your solution, to retention, where they commit long-term. We will provide a number of creative ways of describing this journey, but your goal is to break down the journey into specific steps. It will be far more detailed than a general-purpose mission statement, making the story of how a customer finds, tries, and continues to use your product come to life.

Product Strategy

Once you have a customer outcome and you've mapped out the customer journey vision, you need a strategy for getting from point A (today's customer journey with your product) to point B (realizing the customer journey vision). Your product strategy works backward from your vision and makes it achievable by accounting for business realities and constraints, identifying the key steps along the way, and establishing measurable milestones to ensure you stay on track.

Application of the Framework

When you've created a product strategy, you will have completed the final piece of the Vision-Led Product Management framework. Next comes the equally important task of implementing it within your company. To do that, in **Part Three** of the book, we will show you how to set smart roadmap priorities that feed into the software development life cycle. We will also cover how to hire the best people, establish appropriate processes, and cultivate a strong culture for ultimately realizing your product vision.

Case Study

STORYBLOCKS:
THE EFFECTS OF VISION-LED
PRODUCT MANAGEMENT

Storyblocks is the world's first stock media subscription service, offering video, audio, and images. We've worked with them since 2015 and as their CEO, TJ Leonard, put it, "We can see and feel Prodify's influence all over Storyblocks." Over that time frame, the company has more than doubled ARR while growing product and engineering to fifty people, representing nearly half of the Storyblocks team.

Over the years, we've helped the Storyblocks team with product vision, strategy, and team development initiatives, but there were a couple of moments that stood out. One was an onsite workshop to create a customer outcome pyramid. Prior to that workshop, TJ shared his thoughts with a few people on the three drivers of customer value (plotted nicely on XYZ axes). After the team brainstormed individually how they would draw the customer outcome pyramid, it became clear that there was great alignment within the team. Working across departments, the team came up with a key outcome that revolved around Storyblocks' aim of "giving all creatives the ability to pursue storytelling without limits." This served as a great foundation as the team went on to think about products and features that would "10x" the customer outcome by improving the efficiency at which customers could create their high-quality video content at scale.

Another example of applying the Vision-Led Product Management framework came from working backward from major milestones to come up with a product strategy. In this case, TJ kicked off the process by providing business outcomes (revenue goals), and we worked with him to draw a strong connection back to the customer value they needed to deliver in order to drive the top-line growth they sought over a five-year horizon. From that point, the product team was able to identify the gaps in the existing product and craft a strategy to fill those gaps to realize their product vision in a way that ensured customer and business outcomes would be aligned in the end.

ANCILLARY BENEFITS OF AN INSPIRING VISION

Having a compelling end-state customer vision can also do wonders for your company when it comes to hiring, employee retention, and fundraising. People want to work for and invest in a company that has an exciting vision, so if you can show people the amazing things you're working toward, they are going to be far more interested and engaged in what you're doing. That's the hidden power of strong product leadership.

Ben's Story

A VISION WORTH SHARING

When I first met James Quigley, co-founder and CEO of GoCanvas, we talked for a while, and at the end of our discussion, he boldly declared that I would work for him one day. I politely told him I appreciated the sentiment but had no plans to leave the advisory practice I'd started.

For the next two years, I advised GoCanvas on several fronts: team growth and hiring plans, organizational structure, product design, and pricing. It wasn't until we began working on a customer-centric product vision that I, as an outsider, finally understood the magnitude of the opportunity for GoCanvas. The product already helped mobile workforces digitize their data collection processes (invoices, inspections, timecards, etc.), and the vision answered the question, "How could we help customers grow their businesses, keep employees safer, and improve the experience for *their* customers by allowing them to do more with the data they are already collecting?"

But it did much more than that. Indeed, the product vision was inspiring enough that GoCanvas became an opportunity I simply couldn't pass up, and though two and a half years earlier, I wouldn't have entertained the possibility, I excitedly joined the company in 2018 as their first chief product officer.

The same vision contributed to a later investment from the top-tier private equity firm K1 and several excellent senior hires. That's the magic of a compelling vision grounded in customer value: it turns heads and changes minds.

The only downside was having to hear James say, "I told you so," while introducing me to the company on my first day.

ACTION CHECKLIST AND RESOURCES

Visit *buildwhatmattersbook.com* for an action checklist, as well as resources about what it means to become product-driven, how to know if your company *is* product-driven, and details on the key concepts of Vision-Led Product Management.

PART

II

CREATING A PRODUCT VISION AND STRATEGY

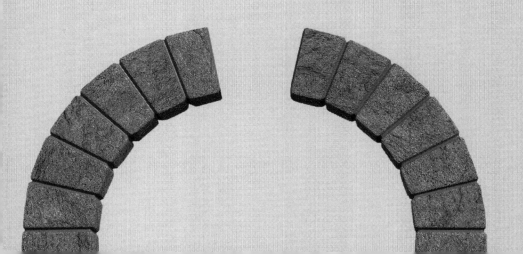

CHAPTER 3

KEY OUTCOMES

"What gets measured gets managed."

—Peter Drucker

I n order to know if you're building what matters, you need to measure what matters. Many product teams strive to be data-driven by measuring the impact of their changes but they've never asked whether the metrics they're tracking are true signals of value delivery. In this chapter, we'll talk about *key* outcomes—not *all* the things customers and the business are hoping the product will do for them, only the *most important* ones. Much of this chapter focuses on the key *customer* outcome because many companies have not yet articulated it, but we will also cover the key *business* outcome to ensure everyone internally is aligned on what product success means.

YOUR CUSTOMERS NEED TO CARE

When most product teams start working on a product vision and strategy, they want to jump directly to the product experience they are going to create, the piles of money they stand to make, or the industry shake-ups their innovations will yield. They skip over the most important question, which is, "What outcomes will my product produce for my customer?" Without an answer to that basic question, nothing else matters. Any dreams of big exits, unicorn status, or market dominance hinge on providing sufficient value to customers.

Too many companies are focused exclusively on their internal metrics. We hear it all the time, "We're going to get to $100 million in recurring revenue! We're going to *disrupt this industry!*" Here's the thing. No one disrupts an industry directly; you disrupt an industry by solving a customer need *so well* that the industry is changed forever.

A product is only ever as good as the value it delivers to customers. For that reason, we encourage you to measure *customer outcomes* in addition to your own internal metrics. At the end of the day, if your customers don't care, all the marketing and sales funnel optimizations and design tricks in the world won't make any difference. It's critical to understand that value, not just from your own perspective as an innovative tech company, but from the perspective of your customer for whom technology is nothing more than a means to an end. How and why would *they* say that the product is beneficial? What would they say to their peers about what they are looking for before they even discover your product? How will they determine whether it is achieving what they expected or hoped?

Ben's Story

HIDDEN SHIPPING COSTS

One of the most fundamental experiences in an e-commerce product is called "finding," in other words, showing buyers the items they're looking for. At eBay, I was product manager on the finding team responsible for the item details page, which showed what sellers listed. Counterparts on my team included product managers for searching, browsing, the bidding flow, and so on. Our team collaborated well, worked hard, and learned a great deal from one another. We also made our share of mistakes.

As we were all data-driven, we wanted to quantify the quality of our search experience so we could improve it over time, so we developed an internal metric: *number of items viewed per search conducted*. The idea was that if a customer ran a search but failed to click on any of the results, we must have missed the mark. However, if a customer clicked on a whole bunch of the items shown, then we must have nailed it. On the surface, this made sense, but we later learned the hard way that it was an awful metric to manage against. Here's why.

At the time, shipping costs weren't shown on the search results page. Buyers could see the price of an item immediately, but they needed to click on the item to see the additional shipping cost, which was only available on the item page. We knew this was an annoying buyer experience because buyers would see what *appeared* to be a great deal, excitedly click on it, then feel disappointed when they saw an exorbitant shipping charge. So they would click the browser back button, return to the search results page, and select the next item, and the next item, and so on. I watched a usability study in which a customer asked for a pad of paper to write down the shipping costs in order to manually add them to the item prices and find the best deal. Ouch!

Making matters worse, sellers who wanted more clicks on their items competed to have the lowest prices displayed on search results. Since they knew shipping costs *weren't* displayed, they realized that the best way to sell their products was to build all of their profit margin into shipping, so they jacked up shipping costs to unreasonably high levels. It wasn't unusual to find brand new DVDs selling for $0.01 with $25 ground shipping.

Why didn't we immediately prioritize displaying shipping costs on search results? The answer was surprisingly simple: we didn't *want* to. We had established the "items viewed per search" metric with our buyers' best interests in mind, and we became devoted to it. We knew that showing high shipping costs would reduce total item clicks, and we didn't want to unravel the progress that had been made through hard work.

Despite the absurdity of this thinking, the logic was sound. The problem lay in the *metric* we were trying to optimize. It didn't directly measure what our customers actually wanted. If we had asked them, no one would have said, "I want to click on as many items as I can every time I run a search." They would have said, "I want it to be fast, easy, and fun to find what I'm looking for." That's what we should have been measuring from the beginning.

Had we framed success from our *customers' perspective*, rather than using our internal lens, we would have quickly come to a different conclusion, fixed what was broken sooner, and delivered a more delightful experience that drove buyer loyalty. Instead, we sent them packing to this other site you may have heard of called Amazon.com.

PRODUCT MANAGEMENT IN A PRODUCT-DRIVEN COMPANY

There is a critical dynamic that product-driven companies need to recognize and use to guide their product development efforts. The dynamic works like this: a company wants to grow its own success metric—typically some way of measuring revenue or profit such as trailing revenue, annual recurring revenue (ARR), or gross margin (GM)—but no matter how hard they try to optimize their own business results, they are constrained by an upper limit, which is the value that the product delivers to customers *as perceived by customers*. In order to grow their own success metrics, companies need to first provide greater customer value.

Most product development work can be classified as either:

- Delivering value to customers (examples: useful features, configurability, usability, cross-device support, speed, and reliability.)
- Extracting value for yourself based on the value delivered to customers (examples: increased prices, more

evolved monetization strategies, attention-grabbing buttons, optimized flows, shorter free trial length.)

What we have found is that most product development teams focus far too much attention on extracting value for themselves and far too little on delivering value to customers. Melissa Perri, CEO of Produx Labs and author of *Escaping the Build Trap*, offers a smart framework for thinking about the relationship between the customer and the business, which she refers to as "the value exchange system." When we spoke with her about it, she explained, "Product-led businesses provide solutions to address customers' wants and needs. Customers will only provide value back to businesses when their wants and needs are actually fulfilled. So, product management must focus first and foremost on delivering outcomes that customers actually care about."

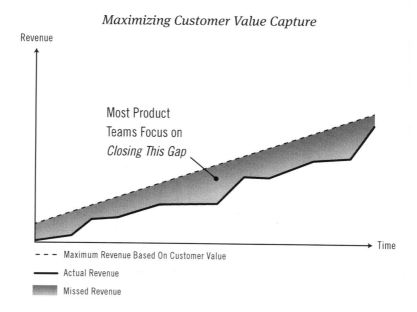

Maximizing Customer Value Capture

As you can see in the above graphic, most product teams focus on closing the gap between the value they *could* capture and the value they *actually* capture. While we consider this to be a major issue in the technology industry, it's not at all surprising that companies end up under-prioritizing customer outcome delivery. There are several reasons for this.

First, there is often plenty of low-hanging fruit available for improving business results in the early days after a new product launches. Unfortunately, this breaks down quickly as the remaining opportunities to drive meaningful internal metric improvements dwindle. When customer value is fixed, the more progress that's made optimizing internal business outcomes, the less room remains for further optimizations.

Second, companies find it easier to measure their own internal business outcomes (such as money in the bank) than the value they deliver to their customers (such as hard-to-measure customer ROI or an even less intangible benefit such as a feeling of security). The famous Peter Drucker quote, "What gets measured gets managed," is generally misunderstood as "whatever is easiest to measure is what we should manage," and that is a flat-out wrong interpretation.

Third, companies don't even realize the trade-off exists. They've become so detached from their customers that they think of them as numbers on a dashboard rather than real people with real desires, capabilities, and constraints. As a result, they end up making an implicit assumption that their product is already good enough for the prospective customers they're attracting. They believe the best way to grow is to remove friction or increase prices. However, in nearly every case, if they were to interview prospective customers who didn't buy to find out why, only a small fraction would cite "friction in the sign-up process" over "perceived value" as the primary reason.

So, companies continue on this convenient yet unsustainable path. After all, their previous work has shown demonstrable ROI, the required product changes are usually faster to implement, and the results are easy to measure using A/B testing.

There will always be room for optimizing business outcomes based on customer value already delivered by the product, but product-driven companies with high ambitions realize that even if it takes more time, the foremost concern is removing the constraint that's hindering growth. That constraint is customer value, which can be expanded by fulfilling a vision that will produce a transformative outcome for the customer. We call this *vision-led value creation*, as you can see it in the top right of the following graphic:

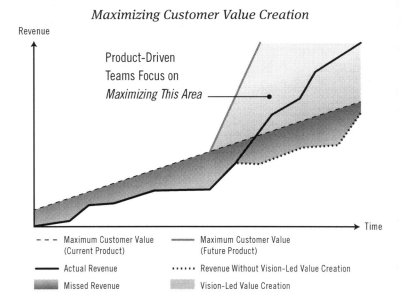

Maximizing Customer Value Creation

A good example of ongoing investment in customer value would be the benefits associated with American Express Platinum membership. They have continued to add new perks beyond airport lounge access and miles through partnerships. As of the writing of this book, they have also included hotel upgrades, credits on Uber, credits for streaming services, ShopRunner memberships, and more. Increasing (and adapting) consumer benefits improves member acquisition and customer retention rates, and it's a better strategy than merely optimizing their web sign-up process or putting up barriers that make it harder for customers to cancel.

Don't attempt to mine for more business results when there are none to be found. If the value you're deriving *from* your customers exceeds the value you're delivering *to* your customers, you put yourself in a dangerous place. Customers may not be getting enough ROI by using your product, which means they are primed to abandon you, in which case, you've created the perfect opportunity for a competitor to swoop in and steal them away. It's the product leader's job to avoid this *product danger zone*, as seen in the following graphic. Jeff Bezos has described this effect rather eloquently in saying, "Your margin is my opportunity."

One of the most common reasons companies find themselves in the product danger zone is that the product manager feels pressured to grow the internal metrics of the company—recurring revenue, higher average revenue per account (ARPA), and so on—in such short order that they forget about the customer's ROI. Many companies are so focused on squeezing as much value as possible out of the "customer sponge" that they keep squeezing as hard as they can even when the sponge is dry. We suggest reversing these priorities by first keeping the sponge sufficiently wet. Obsess over maximizing the value your product delivers to customers, and only then consider how you can better monetize that value without stressing about whether you've squeezed out the last drop.

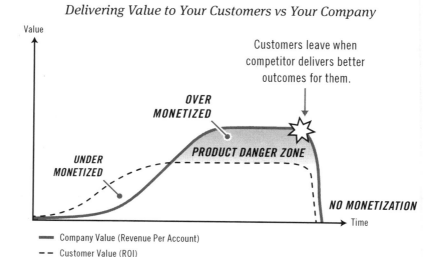

Delivering Value to Your Customers vs Your Company

DRIVING BUSINESS RESULTS VIA CUSTOMER OUTCOMES

Financial results and business outcomes are absolutely critical, and we are not suggesting that customer outcomes are somehow more important. They go hand in hand. However, providing customer value is what creates the *opportunity* to produce sustainable financial outcomes for the company, not the other way around. It's the responsibility of product management to create a product that is both valuable to customers *and* highly profitable for the business. By focusing on customer outcomes, you will be in a position to generate greater business results over time.

Of course, getting strong financial returns is not an automatic result of delivering great customer outcomes. It also requires a smart pricing strategy, ongoing optimization, and a lot of good old-fashioned hard work. Figuring out how to convert customer value into business value is an important part of the product vision and strategy, but it's a problem that's easier to solve than creating customer value when there isn't any.

Balancing customer value and business results is a team sport, and each role in the organization needs to play their position. The product team ensures the product delivers real customer value and can do so profitably, and the go-to-market teams derive as much business value as they can based on the potential customer value inherent in the product. Sales and marketing are usually capable of driving *business outcomes* on their own without product changes. However, it is very difficult for those teams to directly deliver *customer outcomes* without assistance from the product team since the majority of customer value in a tech company is provided by the product directly. This is why the product team's attention should generally be focused on increasing customer value: it's something *only they can do*.

The second division of labor between product and operational teams has to do with how far into the future their activities should be focused. In a product-driven company, product management isn't focused on the short-term goal of hitting numbers this quarter. Instead, product management is focused on *making it possible* to hit much bigger numbers multiple quarters or even years out. In a product-driven company, product management owns the far future. They do so by identifying the real value drivers for customers and bringing them to life in the product, which creates opportunities for their teammates in the go-to-market teams to reap the rewards.

- Customer success and account management maintain and expand revenue from existing customers.
- Sales closes deals in the pipeline to build the customer base and revenue stream.
- Marketing tells the story to the market and builds a pipeline of prospects.

Product management works even farther ahead of marketing to envision a product that marketing can tell a story about. The following graphic shows the time frames each team should be focused on to shape the future of the company.

Ownership of the Company's Future by Team

TODAY	1-3 MONTHS OUT	3-6 MONTHS OUT	BEYOND
CUSTOMER SUCCESS & ACCOUNT MANAGEMENT	SALES	MARKETING	PRODUCT
Grow accounts and get renewals	Close deals in the pipeline	Tell the story, build the pipeline	Create future value

*Timeframes vary by company, product, and business model

CHOOSING THE KEY CUSTOMER OUTCOME

In order to deliver customer value in the long run, you must choose a specific outcome—a *key customer outcome*—to focus your attention on. You will use this key outcome as the focal point for the product vision you later develop, as well as a way to measure your progress delivering value to your customers.

The Driving Force behind Demand

The key customer outcome is the *driving force* behind the demand for your product. It's not *how* they use it, but *why* they use it, and how they will determine whether they should continue using it. Think about what customers actually want by using your product.

- People don't use Twitter to read posts, but to *feel connected.*
- People don't use Peloton to cycle, but to *stay in shape.*
- Employees don't use Google Docs to type words, but to *collaborate.*
- Companies don't use Salesforce to track sales pipelines, but to *close more deals.*

Identifying the key outcome for a product is about getting to the heart of the value the product delivers for the customer. It's important to choose an outcome that customers care about and will be willing to sacrifice something for (money, time, etc.), giving you confidence it will also drive results for your business.

Qualitative Outcomes

In our advisory work, we are often asked whether the customer outcome must be quantifiable. Ideally, it will be directly measurable, but depending on the product and the market, the key customer outcome may be more conceptual or even emotional in nature, and that's okay. If you do choose a qualitative out-come, you can either quantify it through periodic customer sentiment surveys (for example, "On a scale of 1-5, how confi-dent do you feel about your personal finances right now?") or by correlating product usage metrics to the qualitative outcome metric (for example, data analysis shows that users who check their Financial Wellness Score every month are much more likely to say they're confident in their personal finances).

Case Study

TEN PERCENT HAPPIER: IMPACT METRICS

Ten Percent Happier is a mobile app that helps people be happier, healthier, and more resilient through meditation. In working with co-founder and head of product Derek Haswell to apply Vision-Led Product Management, his team ran into an interesting challenge. While customers love the product and recognize the positive impact it has on their lives, defining a specific key outcome proved difficult. The company knew that usage metrics like daily active users (DAU) were too internally focused. Product manager Eva Breitenbach came up with an elegant solution for how to better define key cus-tomer outcomes by looking at impact metrics.

The team ran surveys of customers who had been using the product for some time and asked a series of questions that would reveal what customers paid the most attention to. Eva measured reactions to specific statements (measured on the scale of "1: strongly disagree" to "7: strongly agree"). Examples of survey questions they asked:

1. Since starting to meditate, I express anger or judgment less frequently
2. Since starting to meditate, I find myself being less reactive in stressful situations
3. Since starting to meditate, I am more accepting of other people's differences

In getting responses to these questions, the team was able to determine the impact that usage of the app drove. By correlating the responses with customer engagement and business success metrics, they were also able to ascertain the key outcomes that customers wanted to achieve. If measurable improvement in a specific outcome correlated closely with their usage and appreciation of the app, then it was something customers clearly cared about.

Multiple Outcomes

Sometimes it's appropriate to have more than one key customer outcome, particularly when you have a complex business model. If your company serves different types of stakeholders, then you will need to create an outcome pyramid for each of them. For example, if you're a marketplace company like Etsy, your user base will consist of both buyers and sellers, and the key outcome for buyers will be different than the key outcome for sellers. In a B2B2C company, where your buyer expects the product to drive large-scale consumer behavior change, we recommend making an outcome pyramid for both the buyer and the consumer to track how each is getting value.

By developing an outcome pyramid for every stakeholder who needs to engage with the product for your company to succeed, you can focus on the most important need of each user. Doing this will also help you make tough trade-off decisions on how best to support each stakeholder's key outcome. For example, the marketplace company may realize they need to either fund two small product teams working in parallel (one for the buyers and one for the sellers) or have one team work on a single stakeholder sequentially (first build for the buyers, then the sellers, then launch).

Rajesh's Story

TOO MANY OUTCOMES

Right before I joined HelloWallet as a senior product manager, the company pivoted from a B2C business model to a B2B2C model, selling our financial wellness products to large companies as an employee benefit. As a part of this transition, I started joining sales calls with our buyers: HR leaders. Of course, the sales team wanted to focus those calls on moving the deal forward, so after I did a product demo, I usually only had time to ask the prospect one question. After some trial and error, I landed on a question that provided the most insight:

If you were to pilot this product with a few employees, what metric would you use to decide whether to expand the benefit to all employees when we come to you at the end of the pilot?

The wide range of answers I heard surprised me:

- Reduce employee stress and absences related to personal finances by helping them build emergency savings and pay down debt
- Increase retirement readiness to create upward mobility at the company (it's hard to get promoted when a bunch of executives can't afford to retire)
- Lower healthcare costs by helping employees understand why a high-deductible health plan is a good option

As I thought about these different answers, I realized that the products we would need to build to deliver on each success metric individually would be drastically different from one another. We had competitors whose products were focused on just one of these outcomes. It was hard to design and build a product that could deliver well on all of them simultaneously, and we also had to match these outcomes to what the employees wanted as their financial goals. For example, most workers don't even think about retirement savings because they're struggling to pay the bills every month.

By talking to prospects, we were able to understand the types of outcomes they expected. From there, we focused on a few outcomes and ensured that sales, marketing, and product were aligned so we were targeting the right buyer and ensuring the product could deliver on the outcomes the buyer expected.

The 10x Outcome

Whether directly measurable or not, you will want to choose a key customer outcome that you can improve dramatically for your customers. If you choose an outcome that you will only be able to improve slightly, then why will your customers care? Facebook didn't create a social media platform that made it just a little bit easier to stay in touch with the exact same people. On the contrary, they designed a platform that allowed people to stay in touch with *hundreds* of friends, acquaintances, and family members in a way that was previously far more difficult, if not impossible. Along with its predecessors, Facebook solved a problem in a radical new way which led to a huge outcome for customers *and* the company.

We like to use the concept of a *10x outcome* as a way of encouraging product leaders to think boldly. *The 10x Rule* was created by leadership guru Grant Cardone as a way of encouraging business leaders to set higher goals and take massive action to fulfill their true potential. Your key customer outcome needs to be something you can impact profoundly, customers will care about, and that will create success for your company when you "10x" it.

CHOOSING THE KEY BUSINESS OUTCOME

In the same way you've chosen the key outcome to track customer value delivery, you'll want to make sure everyone at the company agrees on the key outcome for the business. How will we measure the health of the business? While it may seem obvious that a financial metric like revenue or profit would be the key business outcome, we've seen enough debates amongst leaders to know this isn't always the case.

For most companies, the key outcome is to increase shareholder value. That typically comes from improving cash flow or profits, and most teams focus on top-line revenue growth. But consider some other questions a team might ask for how best to increase shareholder value:

- Should we focus on growing revenue through new customers or retaining and upselling existing customers?
- Is there a unique data asset we can build that changes our company's valuation?
- Is there a high ROI on investing in other intangibles like our brand, customer relationships, and team?

Why is it so important to align on the key business outcome? In our experience, we've found that most debates about product priorities stem from a fundamental disagreement on what product success means. Sales thinks it's about closing deals, customer success thinks it's about NPS, engineering thinks it's about the technical quality of the product, and the CEO thinks it's about hitting commitments made to the board. While all of these might be the right outcome at some point, they can't all be the right outcome simultaneously. The product development team is always time-constrained. Getting aligned on how to "keep score" before proceeding any further will minimize friction as you establish your product vision and strategy.

DEVELOPING OUTCOME PYRAMIDS

You've no doubt seen the many dashboards out there that measure an innumerable quantity of internal metrics like revenue, engagement scores, and so on, such as in the dashboard concept shown here. The prospect of digesting all of these metrics to figure out what your customers actually care about or what product changes to make can seem daunting.

A Typical SaaS Product Dashboard

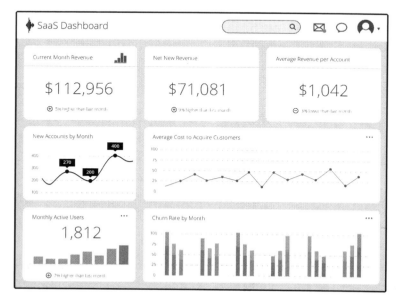

As an alternative to this type of dashboard, we recommend creating what we call a *customer outcome pyramid*. Once you've identified the right customer outcome metric for your product, you can break it down into its constituent parts. We like the pyramid structure because:

1. It forces teams to define the relationship between metrics. A pyramid helps you see which metrics are leading indicators (the bottom of the pyramid) versus lagging indicators (the key outcome at the top of the pyramid).
2. It limits the number of metrics that need to be tracked (the pyramid can only get so wide).
3. It helps you visualize and contextualize metrics that require attention (for example, focusing on improving specific metrics over some time period).
4. It lets you delegate specific product metric goals to individual product managers as the product team grows.

For the customer of a typical B2B SaaS product, the customer outcome pyramid might look something like this:

A B2B Customers's Key Outcome Pyramid

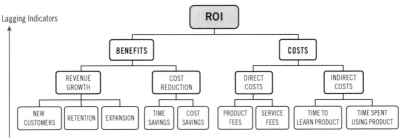

In this example, the overall goal—what customers are look-ing for—is good ROI, and the pyramid shows how the benefits of the product outweigh the costs. That key customer outcome is the top of the pyramid, and the next level then breaks this outcome into *benefits* and *costs*, which are then further broken down into categories and then specific dimensions.

The left side of this ROI pyramid focuses on the benefits your product drives for the customer. Will you help them grow top-line revenue more efficiently? An example of a product that does this is HubSpot's Marketing Automation, which sends automated emails to help convert leads to customers. Will you help customers cut costs by saving time? An example of a prod-uct that does this is Mixmax's one-click meetings, which saves time by replacing back and forth emails to schedule meetings with people outside of your company with a web app that lets those people see your availability and pick a date and time that works for them. Note that there might be other benefits you can deliver to customers that aren't shown in this example pyramid, such as regulatory compliance or reduced data security risks.

The right side then breaks down the costs. First, there are direct costs, such as paying for the product. Then there are indirect costs, such as the time and money it takes to launch the product, learn it, and use it to realize it's true value. By breaking down both benefits and costs to specific dimensions, you get a clear picture of how well you're meeting the customer's key outcome.

When we worked at Opower, a company operating in the sus-tainability space, our key customer outcome was the cost per kWh saved in residential energy usage. Our utility buyers used this metric to compare Opower's behavioral energy efficiency program to other programs, such as LED light bulb installation. Our utility clients' ROI came down to:

- The benefit of cost savings (if millions of households used less energy, the utility didn't have to pay to generate that electricity)
- The costs of the Opower behavioral energy efficiency program (in addition to an ongoing subscription, there was also an up-front integration fee to send us energy usage data)

Note the product implications of this: if we wanted to increase our product price, it had to deliver more energy savings. Otherwise, the ROI could drop so much that we looked less attractive than other energy efficiency programs.

THE DURABILITY OF OUTCOME PYRAMIDS

Because outcome pyramids represent the set of metrics you'll use as a team to measure the value of your product to both customers and your business, they should remain relatively stable. After all, nobody likes a moving target, and changing team goals becomes harder as the team grows in size. We recommend asking yourself whether the pyramids you built could be used for two to three years. Would customers still consider the outcome pyramid valid at that time? Have you included all the business metrics you want to capture over that time horizon?

If you're not sure whether your outcome pyramids might change over time, consider "zooming out" and creating a bigger outcome pyramid. For example, if the team felt it was a toss-up between two key customer outcomes, you could create a single pyramid that has both outcomes laddering up to a third outcome, then let the team know that for the foreseeable future only one outcome is the focus. As an example, consider how Uber's key customer outcome appears to be moving *anything* more efficiently. They have gone from moving *us* from point A to point B to moving your takeout to your front door to moving you around city blocks. Had the key outcome only been to save time driving, they might never have launched UberEats or JUMP scooters.

THE PROCESS IN ACTION

To illustrate the process of creating your customer outcome pyramid, we will use a fictional SaaS startup we've created called Chuckwagon, a company whose vision is to help users prepare and serve home-cooked meals. We've intentionally chosen a B2C example for simplicity; you'll see later how this gets more complicated with a B2B or B2B2C business model. Through interviewing customers, Chuckwagon learns that their primary frustration is the amount of time it takes to get a home-cooked meal on the table, so they select "time spent on meals" as their primary customer outcome metric.

By creating an outcome pyramid, Chuckwagon can take this primary customer outcome and begin to break it down into specific needs. How are customers spending their time when preparing a home-cooked meal? First, there is planning time, which further breaks down into meal planning and grocery shopping. Then there's cooking time, which breaks down into cooking and cleaning. From there, the pyramid gets into even more specific steps, such as grocery travel time and prep time.

Customer Outcome Pyramid for Chuckwagon

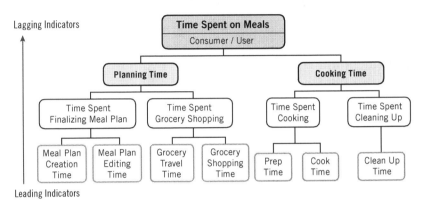

By breaking these tasks down, they've defined the specific dimensions of value creation they can use to meet the key customer outcome. Now, they can work on the features of their product that will provide value to the customer from the customer's perspective.

To balance this consideration, Chuckwagon also creates an outcome pyramid from the company's perspective. The company's primary desired outcome is revenue growth, specifically annual recurring revenue (ARR).

Chuckwagon's ARR breaks down into two revenue streams that are derived from the customer outcome pyramid "branch" of saving time planning meals: paid app subscriptions and grocery delivery. App subscriptions further break down into app downloads and the number of people upgrading from free to paid accounts. Again, the point of this pyramid is to break down the company's primary outcome into specific dimensions of value creation—this time from the company's perspective. By doing so, the relationship between specific metrics in the company's revenue is clarified for everyone.

Business Outcome Pyramid for Chuckwagon

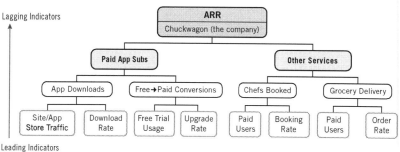

Comparing the two outcome pyramids also reveals the potential synergies between customer outcomes and business outcomes. For example, Chuckwagon might find that grocery delivery adoption helps the company boost revenue and retention, which are both important for the company pyramid, and that it also further saves time for customers, contributing to their key outcome. Setting the level of development effort aside, offering grocery delivery (or partnering with an existing grocery delivery platform) would seem like a smart idea for Chuckwagon to include in their end-state vision.

Developing a bold vision for the customer journey to deliver these key outcomes is the next major pillar of the Vision-Led Product Management framework, which is covered in chapter four.

ACTION CHECKLIST AND RESOURCES

Visit *buildwhatmattersbook.com* for an action checklist and additional resources, such as a worksheet and template to identify your key customer outcome and create your customer and business outcome pyramids.

CUSTOMER JOURNEY VISION

"You cannot depend on your eyes when your imagination is out of focus."

—Mark Twain

O ften, companies will do the work of establishing a primary outcome metric for their customers but then stop there, thinking they're done. Choosing the outcome alone is insufficient. You're not simply aligning your teams around a 10x customer outcome—you also need to define a customer experience that will actually generate that outcome, one that maps an actual *customer journey* that will yield the 10x outcome you want to deliver. This is the foundation of product leadership.

Let's start with a thought experiment. Reset the clock back to the year 2000. Investors bet on you starting a company with a stated goal of "enabling the average consumer to drive wherever they want without ever having to stop at a gas station." You're excited to begin, so you hire several experts who are all working toward that common goal. But there's a problem. While your definition of success is clear, there is no vision for what the actual driving and refueling experience should be, so different teams take different approaches.

One team begins research on a nuclear reactor that can fit in the trunk of a car. Another works on an autonomous gasoline refueling system capable of refueling cars on the go. A third team works on developing an electric battery that lasts the entire lifetime of the car, and a fourth team, inspired by lean design principles and *The Flintstones*, removes the engine entirely and just cuts a couple of holes in the floor of the cab. On top of that, each marketing director has their own ideas, and some sales leaders want to use traditional dealership models, while others think the car should only be sold online. It's an unmitigated disaster!

This is obviously an extreme case used to illustrate the point. In your company, this problem would be more subtle, but team members being even mildly disconnected can yield similarly catastrophic results. In our work as advisors, we see this happen *all the time*. Founders feel they have provided a "vision" of customer success because they've repeated a two-sentence description of the outcome they hope to achieve, but when we ask other employees—even the senior-most executives—to describe the core product capabilities or the key elements of a customer's experience discovering, buying, and using the product, we either get shoulder shrugs or, worse yet, detailed descriptions that are completely different from what everyone else has to say.

There are so many ways to achieve a specific outcome that teams can easily end up pulling in skewed or opposing directions, wasting a tremendous amount of time, energy, and resources. Therefore, once you've selected the right customer outcome, the next step is to clarify all the key elements of the product vision through the lens of the customer engaging with it. It's important to describe all stages of the customer journey, so your team is unified around an outline of a solution that is both actionable and achievable.

Returning to our previous example, instead of simply telling your company, "We're going to design a car that never needs to go to the gas station," and letting your teams spiral off in a dozen different directions, you provide a realistic vision of the customer journey to guide decision-making in a way that is achievable. Founded in 2003, Tesla unified around a specific solution: a battery-powered car with a reasonable range that could be recharged efficiently at home or in select roadside locations. As of the writing of this book, Tesla is the most valuable US car manufacturer of all time.[1]

The communication method matters nearly as much as the content of the customer journey vision itself. Some of the companies we work with have a vision in theory, but instead of writing it down, it's merely shared verbally and operates almost like folklore. It's more effective to transform that folklore into a visual communication tool that everyone can understand, ask clarifying questions about, and eventually rally around. Rather than simply creating a long document that your teams might

---

1   Karen Langley, "Tesla Is Now the Most Valuable U.S. Car Maker of All Time," *The Wall Street Journal*, Jan. 7, 2020, https://www.wsj.com/articles/tesla-is-now-the-most-valuable-u-s-car-maker-of-all-time-11578427858.

not read, we recommend using visual artifacts, which we'll talk about later in this chapter.

How much detail should be included in a product vision? It's a bit of a balancing act. We recommend including enough detail about the customer journey to be confident that disparate teams will be able to align to a cohesive workstream. A clear vision of the customer journey—from beginning to end—prevents you from overlooking one of the steps that might make or break the product's success in the market. However, it's also possible to provide *too much* detail, which could result in either:

- Forcing a specific solution that should be adapted based on customer discovery and validation, or
- Limiting the potential creativity and ingenuity of the teams tasked with bringing the customer journey vision to fruition.

As you think about creating your product vision, here are some of our best practices.

Best Practices for Creating a Product Vision

 Write it down

 Include all elements of the customer journey

 Be bold

 Ensure competitive differentiation

 Determine your time horizon

 Communicate it clearly

WRITING IT DOWN

While this may seem obvious, we find many companies rely on their vision being communicated verbally, which creates several issues:

1. There is no single source of truth. Every time the vision is communicated, it is likely expressed differently, creating confusion through inconsistency.
2. There is no way to reference it later. This means employees will be forced to rely on their memories in times when the vision should be a guiding light. Examples of these times include when explaining the company direction externally, when making important strategic decisions and when trying to inspire their colleagues.
3. There is no easy way to highlight changes. As the vision morphs, the lack of documentation makes it harder for everyone to know the latest version of the vision and how it differs from previous versions.

So a simple best practice is to capture the vision as an artifact that everyone can read, reference, and comment on.

BEING BOLD

A customer journey vision should be bold and transformative. This requires thinking in new ways about how a 10x customer objective can be delivered. To clarify, we're not saying your outcome has to be a specific number that is literally 10x higher. We're simply using "10x" as shorthand for delivering an outcome that is radically different or obviously superior to what has come before. Tesla didn't make a car that was slightly faster to gas up or burned fuel just a little more efficiently.

Marty Cagan, founder of Silicon Valley Product Group and author of the influential product management book *Inspired*, believes most companies need to think bigger when it comes to their product vision. He offers the following advice: "Your product vision needs to inspire. Focusing attention on customer and user value makes your vision truly meaningful, and it has the potential to evoke missionary-like passion throughout your product organization. Avoid the temptation to think in time frames that are too short; it's okay for your product vision to require a leap of faith. In fact, if you are able to fully validate your vision, then you're probably not being ambitious enough in the first place." We wholeheartedly agree.

All of this requires a great deal of creativity and willingness to test the limits of an executive team's tolerance for risk. It's hard to describe methods for brainstorming that will work for every team. However, we do have several recommendations.

1. Create a culture in which ideas are respected throughout the organization. Hear people out, no matter their title, paygrade, or experience in product development. We've previously run "innovation days" in which team members drop their normal daily activities and break out into self-organizing teams to work on a problem they are passionate about solving. Their ingenuity

goes on full display in the end-of-day demo where they showcase to the company what they've conceived of.

2. Conduct a teardown of competitors' products, highlighting all of their weaknesses and the opportunities for them to be disrupted. Don't just look at what they are attempting to do but they execute poorly. Also, pay attention to what they are *not doing at all*. For example, the founders of Opower realized early on that every single energy efficiency solution being sold to utilities was a replacement of a physical product with a new one that was more energy-efficient—like replacing an incandescent bulb with an LED bulb. *No one* was looking at changing how these products were used by the consumer, such as getting them to turn the lights off more often. Consider what your competition isn't doing but should be.

3. Look outside of your industry to another that is changing rapidly and is on the forefront of innovation. Consider the new dynamics that are being created and ask how those same dynamics could be applied to deliver better outcomes for underserved customers in your industry. How could social networking be applied to the medical industry? How could touchscreen interactions be transformative in architectural design?

4. Identify your "unfair advantage" and ask yourself how it can be exploited to the maximum extent possible.

For example, if you have proprietary data no one else possesses, how could that data be used to create an unrivaled customer experience? If you don't have an unfair advantage, ask yourself which one you wish you had and why, and consider how feasible it is to acquire it. Perhaps it should still be part of your customer journey vision.

5. Observe the behavior of potential customers in your target market, not just as they use their current solutions, but before and after they use them as well. Look for inefficiencies that arise from using multiple tools that don't work well together. Are they copying and pasting content from one system into another, manipulating data in the new system, and then copying and pasting the results back into the original one? Plenty of people do this between email, Google Docs, Excel, project management tools, and their own personal to-do lists. There's certainly an opportunity for 10x value creation in the intersection of those spaces.

6. Get employees thinking out of the box with a design thinking exercise to brainstorm customer experiences that will achieve your 10x outcome. Pose a question like this to product, design, engineering, and other team members: "Imagine we had literal superpowers and could bend the laws of physics. How might we solve this customer problem better?" After they answer that question, follow up with, "Since you don't actually have

superpowers, how could you approximate what you just did?" This can help them begin thinking bigger and bolder than they thought possible.

DETERMINING YOUR TIME HORIZON

You want your product vision to be bold, novel, and exciting, but it also has to be realistic and achievable, so you need to set a time horizon that is appropriate given business realities. As a default, we recommend setting your time horizon for three years, because that gives you enough time to think long-term. A three-month vision isn't really a vision, so you want to think far enough into the future that you have space to think boldly and have time to achieve something meaningful.

While three years is a good starting point, your particular circumstances might necessitate a shorter or longer view. There is no magic formula for determining the right horizon for a customer journey vision, but there are multiple factors that should influence the judgment call you'll need to make.

For example, if you're a startup with a ten-month financial runway, then your vision probably shouldn't go far beyond two or three years. On the other hand, if you're an enterprise company, a five-year horizon may be more appropriate since building on your existing product and changing the way you solve customer problems will likely be a more complex undertaking than it would be for a startup.

Maybe your market is evolving rapidly, so you need a shorter time horizon to avoid making a set of assumptions that may not turn out to be true. Think of a digital camera company operating in the early days of smartphones when customer expectations for phone cameras were constantly shifting. In that case, a shorter time horizon would have made sense, as innovative companies attempted to stay ahead of the curve.

On the other hand, if you're operating in the oil and gas industry, your basic product isn't going to change all that much, so you can probably extend your time horizon, confident that the market will adapt more slowly.

Consider changes in your market, but pay equal attention to the things that *won't* change. While you can't predict the future, you can certainly take into consideration how stable things are likely to be within a select period of time. It's possible that you're operating in a space where customers will have the same basic need a decade from now, in which case you can plan farther out.

In "The Institutional Yes," a 2007 case study published in *Harvard Business Review,* Jeff Bezos talks about how he challenged each of his executives to come up with a ten-year strategy for the company.[2] They came back with all sorts of radical ideas, each of which were based on assumptions about future market trends such as, "We believe mobile technology is going to do this. We believe Web 3.0 will be defined as that," and so on.

A frustrated Bezos noted that all of these strategies were based on guesswork. "What happens if the guesswork is wrong?" he asked. "Then our strategy ends up being wrong." He explained that he would rather create a strategy based on things they were

---

2   Julia Kirby and Thomas A. Steward, "The Institutional Yes," *Harvard Business Review, October 2007, https://hbr.org/2007/10/the-institutional-yes*

confident about, customer needs that would almost certainly remain the same: wide selection, great prices, fast delivery, phenomenal customer support. That's what customers wanted a hundred years ago, it's what they want today, and it will probably be what they want ten or twenty years from now.

"How do we build the right products based on the customer needs that are unlikely to change?" he asked. By aligning their thinking to the things that were unlikely to change within their time horizon, he was able to get his team thinking in a direction that led to successful products like the Kindle.

As a best practice, no matter your industry, we feel a roughly three-year vision establishes a nice balance between driving smart decisions affecting your business more immediately and creating value with 10x outcomes over the long haul. You'll want to give yourself enough runway to think creatively about long-term solutions, but not so much runway that it's likely the problem will change while you're in the middle of solving it. Nobody wants to create a solution only to discover that customers stopped caring about it while it was being developed, nor do you want to chase a solution with such a long-term vision that your business can't survive long enough for you to achieve it.

Talk with your engineering and design teams to make sure your time horizon is feasible. Much of that depends on how much risk you're willing to take on. Maybe the vision is feasible but not the timeline, or maybe the timeline is feasible but only if you put more people on the initiative. You can also conduct some feasibility studies, get a few estimates, and make necessary adjustments to either the vision or the time horizon, but if you're overly cautious, your vision is likely to become shortsighted and paltry. On the other hand, if your vision is too grand, too long-term, or not grounded in reality, you may never get there—or you may overlook opportunities for progress through step changes that are still transformative.

Achieving your vision won't happen all at once; it will require some refueling along the way. In the next chapter, we will discuss building checkpoints on the path to realizing your vision. For now, let's focus on setting the destination and a realistic time frame for getting there.

Rajesh's Story

TIME HORIZONS AND FINANCIAL RESULTS

After Morningstar acquired HelloWallet, there was a grand vision for how our two products would come together to provide even more value to consumers and clients. HelloWallet had a product portfolio of web and mobile apps that helped consumers improve their financial wellness, which was offered as an employee benefit. Morningstar's Retirement group also had an employee benefit product portfolio: a set of robo-advisors that used Morningstar's Total Wealth methodology to regularly rebalance an employee's 401(k) to increase the chances of hitting their retirement income goal. The two products seemed like a great bundled offering—as an employee climbed what we called the "financial wellness ladder" by building emergency savings and paying down debt, it would be great to offer a simple way to sign up for the robo-advisor once they had put their first dollar into the employer-sponsored retirement savings account. However, we ran into a couple of issues related to the time horizon for this bundled offering.

First, since neither product was designed to be bundled with the other, the vision was to create a third product that combined the two feature sets together. Like many enterprise projects, this had a timeline of roughly two to three years. However, there were no technical estimates to validate if it was feasible. When we started producing the estimates, we realized that a couple of tech replatforming initiatives would be required to create an integrated product, pushing it to more like a seven- or eight-year vision. This was a problem because our revenue projections assumed this work would happen in two to three years.

Second, we ran into an issue with the user's time horizon. Of course, everyone wants to be able to improve their financial wellness ASAP by building savings and paying down debt. We started thinking about the implications of it taking users a *long* time to work their way up the "financial wellness ladder." Most Americans can't even afford a $500 emergency, so building up a few hundred dollars in emergency savings would take them many months, if not a year or more.[3] It's the same with freeing up enough cash to pay down credit card and

---

3   Quentin Fottrell, "Nearly 25% of Americans have no emergency savings," MarketWatch, June 9, 2020, https://www.marketwatch.com/story/nearly-25-of-americans-have-no-emergency-savings-and-lost-income-due-to-coronavirus-is-piling-on-even-more-debt-2020-06-03

student loan debt. By the time employees had worked their way up to thinking about saving for retirement, it would have taken many years. Users would have likely lost patience, and the business value would not have materialized fast enough.

In the end, Morningstar sold HelloWallet's financial wellness product to KeyBank, a large client whose retail banking product strategy revolved around differentiating through a focus on financial wellness.

ELEMENTS OF A CUSTOMER JOURNEY VISION

A *customer journey vision* is a story detailing the future customer journey you aim to enable to deliver the 10x outcome within the time horizon you set. It includes all the major stages of the customer's journey from the moment they recognize an opportunity for a better outcome until they decide to engage and continue to engage with your product.

Many companies create customer journey visions that only cover a few parts in the middle of the story, overlooking vital steps at the beginning and end, so make sure your vision covers all of the major decision points for your customers, which are outlined next. Of course, some companies will have additional steps depending on their product or service, but at a minimum, your customer journey should include the following stages, where the customer makes a decision about your product before moving on to the next stage:

Customer Journey Stages

TRIGGER   DISCOVERY   EVALUATION   TRIAL   ENGAGEMENT   RETENTION

When crafting your customer journey vision, remember that breadth is more important than depth, so don't worry about diving too deeply into each stage of the journey. However, each stage needs to be described in *sufficient* detail to confirm that the journey you craft is plausible. A good customer journey vision will stand up to reasonable critique without relying on vagueness. It can't be full of questionable assumptions about customer preferences or dubious predictions about user behavior, and it is only as strong as its weakest link. Let's look at the essentials for each of the major stages.

Stage 1: Trigger

Most product teams we talk to believe the customer journey begins at the point a user first interacts with their product, but there's an important stage before that. In the beginning, the customer may not know about your product. The trigger is the point at which the customer begins looking for a new solution to the problem your product attempts to solve. Something has to make them realize that their current solution isn't good enough. This stage sets the context for the overall customer journey, as well as the customer's *mental model*, which is the way they will think about your product and understand its value. Just getting customers to realize that they can have a better solution is often half the battle.

According to behavioral science expert Nir Eyal, there are two types of triggers: internal and external.

Internal triggers are based on impulse. Hunger is a good example of an internal trigger. You don't need to be reminded you're hungry, and the urge to eat is automatic. Some tech companies rely on internal triggers for their product adoption and engagement. If you're feeling hungry (and lazy), you are triggered to find food, which could be in the fridge, down the street, or delivered via an app like GrubHub.

External triggers are based on stimuli. Something grabs your attention and notifies you about a possible change in behavior that you might consider. A pop-up ad, an email landing in your inbox, an alert on your phone, or someone telling you about a new product they just bought are all examples of external triggers. External triggers are more easily manipulated but less powerful than internal triggers that are tied to emotion.

By identifying which type of trigger will kick off your customer journey vision, you can understand the customer's state of mind, which is critical for optimizing the rest of the journey. Returning to the GrubHub example, the fact that the internal trigger of hunger is likely to drive product usage, GrubHub needs to make sure that food can actually be delivered in under an hour, which shapes nearly every aspect of the product and service from the ordering interface to the types of restaurants they have relationships with to the way deliveries are queued. For a catering app, by contrast, hunger is never the trigger, and it changes everything about the customer's journey and the product solution.

You can also include in your customer journey vision how you intend to *manipulate* those triggers to expand demand for your product. For an internal trigger, this requires building deep associations to emotions or routines. External triggers like ads can be bought with marketing dollars, but they can also be created through product-led growth.

Let's consider a cybersecurity example. Many company leaders may not choose to prioritize upgrading their data security until there's a security breach, so they're unmoved by ads about data security solutions, assuming their security is sufficient. To get around this, many smart cyber-security companies have begun to offer freemium products that scan a user's system for security vulnerabilities and then present the results in dramatic fashion. In this case, the trigger might be an ad to run a free scan.

"Oh, my gosh, we have twenty-six data security vulnerabilities," the customer will say. "A hacker could steal our data easily. Maybe we need to do something about this!" Suddenly, the customer realizes they have a problem that the company's solution might be able to solve—an external trigger that begins the customer journey.

Ideally, the trigger event is something you will seek to control or guide in your customer journey vision, rather than simply waiting for that moment to happen spontaneously. What will make a customer realize an outcome is not being met the way they would like? What will make them realize their current solution isn't good enough? Detail this as the first stage of your customer journey vision.

Rajesh's Story

THE BEHAVIORAL SCIENCE
BEHIND TRIGGERS

I had no idea what behavioral science was until I joined Ben at Opower. There, I learned that our entire company was founded on a behavioral experiment by Dr. Robert Cialdini, who found that the most effective way to get people to reduce their home energy usage was to tell them they were using more than their neighbors. This peer comparison was more effective than any message about saving money or the environment.

When I went on to HelloWallet, I had the pleasure of working with Dr. Steve Wendel, our principal behavioral scientist, on how to use behavioral science to improve financial wellness using his CREATE behavioral funnel (Cue, Reaction, Evaluation, Ability, Timing, Experience). In working with Steve, I realized that I was only focused on the execution step: the act of clicking a button, logging in, or completing some task that would improve the user's financial wellness. When we started thinking about how a user might discover a new feature (the "Cue") or decide whether to try it (the emotional "Reaction" and deliberative "Evaluation"), we saw better results. We started sending more product update emails and using a banner message at the top of the home page to direct users to new features. While this may seem obvious, I still see plenty of product teams make the same mistake: not giving the cue to encourage a particular action within the product. Unlike the movie *Field of Dreams,* "if you build it, they will come" never applies to products.

If you'd like to learn more about Steve's CREATE framework, or others like BJ Fogg's (which also focuses on triggers), check out the resources link at the end of this chapter.

Stage 2: Discovery

This second stage is where the customer learns that your product exists, and they begin to associate your solution with their problem. It's all about awareness of your product so it can be in the consideration set.

For example, your car has been giving you trouble for a while, but finally, you experience a breakdown that is going to cost a ridiculous amount of money to repair. At this point, you realize, "I need a new car!" That's the trigger. But what makes you choose specific dealerships to visit? It might be the result of TV advertising, local sports team sponsorships, or signage that you drive past every day while heading to work. What makes you consider certain makes and models but not others? The reputation of the car manufacturer, reviews on public forums, the projected resale values, and most notably, the brand associations you've built up over the years and word-of-mouth conversation, all contribute to your behavior in the discovery phase.

The automaker Genesis consistently gets the highest ratings from its customers, yet as of the time of this writing, it is a poorly recognized brand that often remains undiscovered when a consumer considers buying a new car. Genesis could invest more into building an even better car to close the deal every time following a test-drive, but it won't matter if no one is test-driving Genesis vehicles in the first place.

Innovative tech companies often find themselves facing one of two very different challenges regarding discoverability:

1. The product is going head-to-head against existing market solutions in a crowded space or one dominated by a monopoly and has to avoid getting lost in the noise.
2. The product is *so new* that the problem it solves is one that potential customers can't recognize, classify, or describe. With no competitors to compare to, they may not be aware of the existence of the product or even the category.

Given the challenge you are facing, how will you get potential customers to make the connection between their desired outcome and your product? How will a customer come to learn that your product exists?

There are many different ways that a potential customer can discover your product, but you need to identify what that step *should* be and ensure you've included it as part of your vision. A B2B company might decide that discovery will occur primarily at trade shows, but in a B2C context, customers don't attend trade shows, in which case advertising might play a bigger role.

Often, the competitive battlefield isn't product quality or features but Google search results. Recognizing the importance of discoverability on search engines, some product teams invest as heavily in search engine optimization (SEO) as in the product itself. Recall that your existing customer base can also drive the discovery of your product, and, indeed, through product-led growth, your existing customers' usage of your product can serve as both the trigger *and* discovery for new prospects.

Think of the Miro example we shared earlier. A Miro customer invites a noncustomer to their shared whiteboard, and suddenly, the noncustomer thinks, "Wow, this is cool. I never realized how convenient this kind of collaborative whiteboard could be. I should look into getting a Miro account of my own."

As you work through this stage of the customer journey, consider the role your product can play in trigger and discovery. This needs to be clearly articulated as you work through the entire narrative of the customer journey.

Stage 3: Evaluation

Once a customer has discovered your solution, they go through a process of evaluating whether or not they want to try it. Maybe they've searched for a solution on Google, found you at the top of the search results, and wound up on the landing page for your product. They have discovered that your product provides a solution to their problem, but now they must decide whether or not they are willing to try it. Every customer will be asking the same thing in the back of their mind, "Am I actually going to invest the time to try the product, or should I move on to the next search result?"

To use the Miro example, the potential customer realizes that a collaborative whiteboard is better than sending emails back and forth, so they now associate Miro with that better solution.

However, in the evaluation stage, they actually begin attempting to understand the product description to see whether or not they want to try it. "Let's see what the whiteboarding process is like here. Is it easy to interact with other users? How much will it cost? Does it provide storage for graphics and video?"

This tends to be a very brief window depending on the product, the buyer persona, how they were triggered, and the context in which the product is discovered, all of which collectively define the user's mental model. However, this stage of the journey is distinct from the discovery and trial steps that bookend it because, in a sense, the potential customer is looking for reasons to *stop wasting their time*. They almost want a valid excuse to reject the product; in this digital age, where we have such easy access to information and alternatives are plentiful, attention spans are very short.

In crafting your customer journey vision, you must be able to articulate why the customer will choose to invest the time and attention to actually try your product after a brief evaluation. What are they going to see in the product experience that will make them decide to take that next step and create an account, agree to a demo with the sales rep, provide personal information, or anything else you want them to do? What immediate objections might they have, and how will you promptly address them?

Going back to the car example, this is the point at which the customer decides to walk around the dealership lot and engage with the salesperson. Think about all of the things that will impact that experience. Is the salesperson schmoozy, overbearing, or demeaning? Are the advertised prices within the customer's range? Are leasing options available? Does the dealership have a good reputation?

We cannot overstate the importance of understanding the thought processes the customer goes through in each of these stages, but especially in the evaluation stage. Have you ever stood at Costco looking at the displays of flat-screen TVs? Most of them are playing the exact same programming, which highlights picture quality. Each TV is merchandised by being placed directly adjacent to another competitive product, so what makes you overlook one TV and concentrate on another? Manufacturers learned through watching consumers shop that it was color saturation—the more brilliant the color, the more eye-catching the screen. A TV could have more HDMI inputs, a better remote control, higher fidelity sound, and so on, but none of it matters if you never stop to investigate those features in the first place.

The irony is that cranking the saturation up high enough to be competitive on the showroom floor makes for an obnoxiously distracting viewing experience at home. So, manufacturers created a new "demo mode" feature for their TVs that is off by default when consumers unpack the box, but that retailers could enable. If you introduced a new TV to the market that had the perfect color display capabilities for viewing at home, you might have the best product, but if you ignore the customer's mental model in the context of the evaluation stage, few will buy it.

What is the equivalent of color saturation for your product, and how does it influence the evaluation stage of your customer journey vision?

Stage 4: Trial

Once customers have decided to give your product a fair shot, what will make them choose to commit to it? If the trigger is a customer's car breaking down, discovery is seeing an article or billboard advertising your company's better car, and evaluation is the customer walking around the dealership lot, then the trial stage is the test drive. As they take the car out on the road, they are highly aware of every aspect of the experience: how responsive the vehicle is, the comfort of the seat, visibility, performance, convenient access to screens, buttons, and knobs. They are getting a sense of what it's actually like to use the product so they can decide whether or not they want to make a long-term commitment.

What are the criteria by which customers will make a purchase decision? What factors will they consider along the way? How will those criteria evolve as they learn more about the product and the use cases it supports? What level of investment do they need to put in? How long will it take them to see early results? What is at risk for them if it fails?

This is where a free trial might come into play. What are the things a customer needs to see during that free trial to elect to upgrade to a paid account? What are the boxes that you need them to check in order to win them over at this stage?

The trial stage ends when the prospect chooses to become a customer. Usually, this entails paying for the product, though for some free products, it may mean making a less black-and-white but equally firm commitment to change behavior to start using the product, perhaps by displacing another solution. That leads to the next stage: engagement.

Ben's Story

THE LITERAL "AHA" MOMENT

Many companies struggle to connect the dots between early user behaviors in the product and later business outcomes like new logo sign-ups, yet understanding how user engagement correlates to business results is essential for making a business case to invest in UX improvements. When I joined GoCanvas as the chief product officer, this was one of my first tasks.

We had some early guesses about the engagement activities that mattered most based on our usage data. For example, we knew that the usage of certain features correlated with higher conversion rates from free trials to paid accounts, but we didn't know how to interpret those results. Did using those features *cause* prospective customers to buy, or were users who were *already convinced* more likely to use those features? To detangle correlation and causation, we needed to do more customer discovery.

We invited people in our target market to come in for in-person studies. We watched them use the product and had them describe their thoughts out loud. Often, they would get stuck or express that they didn't understand what they were doing as they were doing it. Then we'd see it—the same thing in study after study. At a certain point, they would lean back in their chair, their eyes would open wide, and they would exclaim something like, "Ohhh, ah, okay! Wow, that's really cool! Yeah, I could imagine all kinds of ways to use this at my company. How much does it cost again?" We could see the wheels turning in their heads. It wasn't the use of some specific feature but having accomplished a specific set of onboarding steps that made the value proposition come alive.

Like many companies, GoCanvas had definitions of a marketing qualified lead (MQL) and a sales qualified lead (SQL), which were used to track and manage prospects through the inbound sales funnel. We called users who completed this sequence of engagement steps "product qualified leads," or PQLs. It was a clean way of quantifying the value of an important *engagement* milestone, and we learned that becoming a PQL was a critical step in the trial phase of the customer journey vision.

Stage 5: Engagement

Customers reach this point after they've committed to your product, whether with money, social capital, or something else. Now, the customer needs to engage with your product to make the most of it. It's the last stage of the up-front investment the customer makes into achieving their outcome. For the car buyer, this is the stage when they are getting to know their vehicle as they use it in their everyday lives, driving to work, to the grocery store, to school. However, for many technology products, a one-time purchase isn't enough to make up for the customer acquisition cost (CAC), so any continued engagement post-purchase that is critical to the customer's long-term success becomes critical to the financial success of the product, too.

As a customer engages more deeply with your product, consider all of the important elements of their journey that will ultimately yield their desired outcomes. Most products have many features that go underutilized, and often customers are not even aware they are available. How will your customers learn about them and apply them to get immersed in your product and maximize the value those features offer? How will your customers get assistance when they need it to avoid any potential stumbling blocks?

Engagement is also often described as "adoption" or "activation." What essential behaviors in your product drive activation? Take the communication and collaboration tool Slack as an example. There are several layers of engagement for an enterprise client. It's not enough to buy the product for a handful of their employees if those employees still default to using email communication. They need to get new employees to run Slack on their browsers or better yet, download the desktop application. Those employees need to use it regularly and eventually adopt it as the default channel for communicating with other employees. The more they use it as a file management system, a search tool, or a broadcasting mechanism, the more deeply those employees engage, and the more value they derive from the product. Consider what your key engagement behaviors are and communicate them as part of your customer journey vision.

Stage 6: Retention

Every customer journey has points at which there's a decision about whether or not to continue using the product. Sometimes these are obvious, such as a lease termination date or a contract renewal date, and other times they are less so, such as when being shown a competitive alternative that makes the customer question whether it's worth switching. Retention is effectively customer loyalty, and it's an essential part of the customer journey. The business impact of poor retention, especially for SaaS businesses dependent on recurring revenue, is severe and can destroy unit economics, growth rate, or both.

An important question to answer in the customer journey vision is, "What are the drivers of customer loyalty?" This question breaks down into two further ones:

1. Are customers actually getting the value they expected from the product?
2. Are customers *aware* that they are getting that value?

Keep in mind the second question is just as important as the first. It's critical that customers *realize* the value the product delivers to them so they don't make an error in judgment by abandoning it. That has to be part of the customer journey, as well. What are the indicators of success the customer needs to see, and how can you make sure your customers see them?

For the majority of B2B products, customer retention is largely dependent on how the customer measures the ROI of your product, so think carefully about what's going to make them want to recommit. For consumer products, customer value is typically less tangible but equally important. What will make a customer think it's a no-brainer to continue using (and paying for) your product?

You need to determine what will make customers want to recommit and what events must be avoided at all costs as they would constitute a trigger event for your customer to switch to an alternative product.

Special Considerations for Your Product

The six stages we've discussed in this chapter are fairly standard in the tech industry, but every product is different. You may have additional stages in your customer journey, or some of the stages we mentioned may not apply to you. For example, many products have upgrade options or ancillary modules that are available midway through a customer's lifecycle, which were not covered earlier.

A marketplace company needs to lay out the customer journey from both the buyer and the seller's perspective. Think about a website like Upwork, which connects people who need jobs done with skilled freelancers. What is going to make a company post a job there, and what is going to make a freelancer look for that job there? You need to describe the end-to-end journey for both groups.

For companies depending on product-led growth, which is really another term for viral growth, your customer journey actually has a loop in it, because once a customer reaches the engagement or retention stage, they are then able to create the trigger moments in new customers. In this way, viral growth loops accelerate the trigger, discovery, evaluation, and trial chapters of the customer journey because they all happen in a few seconds. The trigger and discovery come from the invitation to use the product, the evaluation happens rapidly if the invitation comes from a trusted source ("well, they must have done some research before picking this product"), and the trial happens in the context of using the product after accepting the invitation.

Take license to redefine the customer journey stages to be appropriate for your product.

ENSURING COMPETITIVE DIFFERENTIATION: THE KANO MODEL

How much focus should you place on competitors? Some people will tell you to ignore them and just go build something great for your customers, while others will say you need to pay special attention to what the competition is doing until you achieve parity.

Of course, if you decided to build a new search engine, ignoring Google would be incredibly foolish because Google has such dominant market share. If you don't deal with the elephant in the room, you're not going to succeed. Even if you're the first in your market, there is always the threat of some new challenger arising to steal your crown. That's exactly what happened to Barnes & Noble when Amazon began its meteoric rise. Did Barnes & Noble simply ignore the threat? Actually, yes, to a large extent they did, and we've all seen the end result.

On the other hand, you can become *too* obsessed with trying to match your competitor, which can end up hindering innovation. Imagine if Amazon in its early years had looked at Barnes & Noble and said, "We need to beat them at their own game, so let's replicate everything Barnes & Noble does. We'll build brick and mortar buildings just like theirs and set up shop next door to their locations, so we can drive them out of business." That probably would not have been a recipe for success, and it certainly would not have achieved the tremendous growth that the company experienced. Instead, Amazon created an innovative new experience for buying books that overturned the status quo and rocketed them past their rival.

The truth is, in certain ways, you need to pay close attention to your competition, and in certain ways, you need to ignore them. Specifically, you need to understand what they're doing so you can intentionally differentiate your product in your customer journey vision. Design your product with your target customer in mind first and foremost, but stepping into their shoes, recognize the other options available to them so you can ensure you're working toward offering a better solution. Have a crystal clear explanation of why your target customer will choose your product over your competitor's. If you don't have a great answer to that question, then yes, it means you need to deal with your competition.

To do this effectively, we recommend using the Kano Model, which clusters your product features based on how they translate to perceived customer value. Developed by quality management expert Noriaki Kano, the Kano Model breaks down product features into specific categories: *must-haves*, *performance features*, and *delighters*. To illustrate the difference between these, we will return to our example of purchasing a car.

Must-Haves

According to the Kano Model, there are certain customer requirements that have to be met in order to compete in the market. Without them, you'll never beat the competition because you don't even get to play the game. For example, if you're design-ing a new car, you might have great engine performance, the smoothest ride in the world, and comfortable seats, but if you lack seat belts, no one is going to buy your car. No one buys a car *because* of the seat belts, but if you were to remove them, sales would immediately grind to a halt.

A basic level of safety, including seat belts, is considered a "must-have" in the market. Sometimes, these requirements are dictated by customers, and sometimes they are dictated *to* cus-tomers by regulations. For example, if you want to do business in Europe and you plan to collect customer data, you have to meet General Data Protection Regulation (GDPR) requirements. Meeting these regulatory requirements might be boring, frus-trating, and annoying, but it's simply not optional.

Performance Features

Once you've met the minimal requirements of the market, you have to surpass the competition in order to win over customers. If you're a vehicle manufacturer, the collection of performance features of your car needs to be better than that of all other cars in the same class for *at least one* group of consumers.

Performance features are those that customers have in mind during the evaluation and trial phase of their journey. In the enterprise space, these are the functional requirements that often appear in a request for proposal (RFP). In the consumer space, you can almost imagine performance features as the items they would put into an RFP if they had to. Customer sat-isfaction scales roughly linearly with performance factors: the better the feature, the more satisfied a customer will be. For a car, these attributes might include gas mileage, reliability, value, handling, safety rating, trunk space, aesthetics, and music playback options. Depending on the persona or segment, the relative importance of these attributes may be dramatically different. Consider what the stereotypical twenty-something might prioritize versus a parent with four school-age kids.

You don't have to create a one-size-fits-all vehicle that is perfect for every single person. Such a thing is not even possible. Different groups of customers are looking for different things. People who love Jeeps want different things than people who prefer sports cars. That's okay. You just have to create the best product for a specific targetable segment within your broader target market.

Keep in mind it doesn't do any good to be second-best for every segment of your target market, losing to a different competitor each time. You need to envision a solution that will be perceived as *best* when compared to all viable alternatives for that market segment, even if that segment is initially only a fraction of the larger market you eventually intend to serve.

Delighters

The last category in the Kano Model is *delighters*, which includes those features that no customer expects, but which they greatly appreciate once they have them. These are the surprises that dramatically enhance the customer experience. It's like buying a new car and realizing it has a few interesting features that you didn't expect. "Wow, this thing has a heated steering wheel for driving in the winter. I love that! It can parallel park itself? That's amazing! I've always hated parallel parking!" While delighters are not part of the list of things that customers are looking for when they seek out your product, they can really set it apart from the competition.

If the discovery phase of your customer journey vision includes hearing great things about your product from word of mouth or product reviews, then you cannot downplay customer delight. Delighters are the features that customers are excited to talk about. No one buys a new car and then tells a friend they love it because, "Those seatbelts really get the job done," or, "The brakes are just so responsive." Instead they talk about the delighters: "I love how the door handles pop out when I get close to the car and retract again after I enter. It's just so cool!"

EVOLUTION OF CUSTOMER EXPECTATIONS

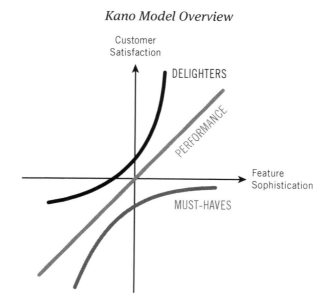

Kano Model Overview

The difference between must-haves, performance features, and delighters has to do with how much customer satisfaction scales for each one. Satisfaction plateaus with must-haves: at some point, you either have it or you don't. Satisfaction scales linearly with performance factors: the more you do, the more satisfied your customers will be (think gas mileage with cars). Satisfaction scales exponentially with delighters: since they're unexpected, a little extra effort can go a long way.

The classification of product features into the three categories is a handy communication tool for understanding how to differentiate when constructing the customer journey vision. Classifications of must-have, performance, and delighters can vary dramatically from one segment of the market to the next. However, it's also important to be aware that the classifications aren't static even for the same customer. Their expectations change over time, and a feature that started out as a delighter or performance feature can quickly become a must-have. When the first commercially available power steering system appeared in Chrysler vehicles in the 1950s, customers didn't really expect the feature. Very few, if any, were demanding it, but once vehicle manufacturers started installing it, customers realized how much they liked power steering.

Now, of course, everyone expects power steering. If you test drove a brand-new car and it lacked power steering, you would think, "What is wrong with this thing? What a horrible driving experience." This happens with delighters and performance features. First, customers are surprised and delighted by them, then they start judging based on them, and eventually, they come to expect them. The same could be said for power windows and automatic transmissions, and will eventually be said for self-driving capabilities.

Innovations that start out as differentiating become normative. That's a major reason why you have to keep innovating. As customer expectations change, new performance features and delighters will emerge in the market. A forward-looking vision needs to account for this evolution in customer expectation.

The first smartphone with both a front and back camera was the Motorola A920, but customers hadn't really been clamoring for this feature. It was a delighter that, at the time, made customers say, "Oh, that's pretty cool. I can take a selfie without reversing the camera." Now, however, a smartphone without a camera on both sides would struggle to find shelf space.

Your goal should be to delight your customers three or five years from now, whatever the horizon of your customer journey vision is. Try to imagine what the *next* "cool feature" should be because today's delighters probably won't be such a big deal by the time you fully realize your customer journey vision.

COMMUNICATING YOUR VISION CLEARLY

Have you ever experienced a vivid dream? Perhaps it made sense right after you woke up, but later in the day, when you tried to explain it to someone, the gaps in the story you hadn't noticed before became obvious. That's the danger of a vision only in your own head, or just communicated verbally. You will be surprised how much still needs to be figured out when you take the time to put it down on paper. After all, what makes sense in your head doesn't always make sense when you write it down and see it in black and white.

Furthermore, a vision is only as good as the degree to which it's understood by those who will execute it. To communicate your product vision clearly, use a format that allows you to work through the stages of the customer journey toward your desired end-state and presents it in an engaging way so that individuals are less likely to develop their own nonconforming interpretations. Often, there is a longer document, either a multipage prose document or a slide deck that covers the crucial customer experiences at each of the key stages of their journey. While the forcing function of documentation can be a very useful exercise, we've learned (the hard way) that most people in the company are too busy to read lengthy documents, and all too often, they collect digital dust on a digital shelf.

For that reason, we recommend the following types of artifacts: *comic strips*, *vision mock-ups*, and *customer diary entries*. We believe they communicate your customer journey vision in the most effective manner so that your team members can wrap their heads around the content. You can choose one of them, all of them, or invent your own.

Comic Strip

We recommend creating a customer journey comic strip that tells the story of your customer as they move through the stages of the journey with your product in a visually appealing and digestible format.

Here's an outline of what a customer journey comic strip might look like for our imaginary product Chuckwagon:

The comic strip format constrains storytelling to individual frames, which naturally emphasizes the most important points in the customer journey. Thought bubbles and speech bubbles show the essential realizations and decisions your customers make along the way. There's insufficient space to get into the weeds of the end-solution, which prevents nitpicky judgments and the potential for distraction from the bigger picture concept. It can also be really fun to piece together!

A comic strip format creates a character-oriented narrative that is highly readable, accessible, and clear. Keep in mind it needs to be holistic, explaining the entire customer journey, not just onboarding and engagement. It should be short, so stakeholders can read it in just a couple of minutes and still get a clear picture. Finally, it should come across as *human*, explaining how the customer *feels* as they discover, try, and use your product. These feelings are hugely important in explaining why someone will adopt your product, the internal motivations pushing them, and the obstacles they must overcome.

Vision Mock-ups

We also recommend creating a set of *vision mock-ups*, which offer a visual representation of what your product could look like. In a sense, vision mock-ups take individual panels in the comic strip and flesh them out. For example, a mock-up might answer the question, "Once a customer has downloaded our app, what will be included in the onboarding experience?"

Bear in mind, the purpose of these visuals is to communicate a high-level concept, so you're not locking your team into a specific implementation. Instead, you are sparking debate so you can generate discussion and get feedback, which a visual does more effectively by providing something tangible for your team to look at and think about.

We understand that people working in an Agile community might balk at the idea of creating mock-ups for something so far in the future. "If you create a mock-up, then the sales team will try to sell it," they might say, "and then you'll be stuck having to build your product in a specific way, but we need feedback from customers along the way for our design work!"

Vision mock-ups are different. Think of them like a concept car that appears on stage at a car show. They present an idea of what you're building toward in a way that people can see, walk around, touch, and talk about, which is healthy, as long as everyone understands their purpose. When BMW reveals a concept car at an industry event, they are not locking their design team into those design specifications. No one says, "Our future car must look exactly like this!"

Remember, these are not deliverables that you will hand to engineering. They are *concept wireframes* that will drive research and point you in the right direction. Marty Cagan refers to these mock-ups as *vision types*, which we think describes their purpose perfectly. If they are shared with customers, they should be positioned as directional and not concrete—again, like a concept car.

Let's take a look at some sample vision mock-ups for our imaginary app Chuckwagon. The key point is that these mock-ups create a concrete, visual way of expressing how Chuckwagon can save time in meal planning, grocery shopping, and cooking.

Household Profile and Meal Planning Features

Grocery List and Delivery Features

Book A Chef Feature

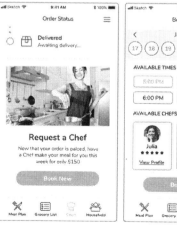

Customer Diary Entries

Another option for describing the customer journey vision is to author an imaginary customer journal where you describe the customer's thoughts and actions throughout the journey in their own words. Approach this as if you were writing an actual diary from the customer's point of view, describing all of their interactions with the product.

Here is an extract from a four-page-long customer diary that Ben used to explain the customer journey vision at GoCanvas in early 2019:

> *January 7th, 2022: I'm sick of all this paperwork. The stack of forms on my desk seems to never end. Why are our internal processes so inefficient and behind the times, anyway? Shouldn't we be handling all of these forms digitally by now? Couldn't some of this work be automated?*

> *January 8th, 2022: I spent the morning on Google looking for something that can turn all of this mind-numbing paperwork into online forms or, better yet, mobile apps. I was surprised to see that there were so many companies claiming to do this. Interesting.*

You are presenting the same narrative as in the comic strip, but this time it's in a prose form that communicates the customer's thoughts and feelings throughout their journey in greater detail. This can be a useful exercise for putting yourself in the customer's mindset, trying to see your product through their eyes, so you're not tempted to make the mistake of communicating the vision in terms of business outcomes.

OPTIONAL COMPONENTS OF A VISION DOCUMENT

There are a couple of optional additions that can help you enrich the customer journey vision: *personas* and *design principles*. Some companies feel these are not necessary parts of their customer journey vision, but we recommend including them in most cases—the more detail you can provide about the customer journey, the less ambiguity will remain to stoke misalignment. Let's take a look at how they can help clarify your product vision.

Personas

A persona is a composite sketch of a specific type of user or buyer within your target market, describing a key segment of your intended audience, including their key outcome, concerns, and decision-making criteria. Depending on the complexity of your industry and the results of your customer research, you may create numerous personas, each encapsulating a unique segment of your target market. There are generally two types of personas: buyer personas and user personas.

Buyer personas describe the person responsible for the decision to buy the product. Their desire for the product is closely tied to the direct outcome they expect to get from the purchase. For example, a VP of customer support might be the buyer persona for a product aimed at helping customer support personnel to be more efficient in taking and logging calls with customers. However, the VP will not be using the product themselves. Buyer personas may have a very different orientation than user personas. Often, the marketing team plays a heavy role in or has direct responsibility for defining and maintaining buyer personas.

User personas describe the person who will be using the product on a more regular basis. The characteristics of user personas help differentiate how they will interact with the product, so their technical ability, attention level, frustrations, and adjacent activities are important to describe as they will influence the customer journey vision. When the user persona is a different person than the buyer persona, as is typical for an enterprise product, users may not care about the buyer's key outcome at all. Instead, they tend to concentrate more on whether the product makes their own lives easier or harder. Consider the difference in how a customer service representative might evaluate a product when compared to the VP of customer support. User personas should be maintained by a combination of product management and design.

For consumer products, the user persona and the buyer persona typically merge together since the same person who will use the product decides to buy the product. Most consumer companies only define user personas since the "user" components of the persona tend to more clearly define and disambiguate groups of customers.

The overall purpose of defining personas is to develop a deeper understanding of how a specific user's orientation will influence their journey. While creating personas is not absolutely necessary at this stage, they are far more important for complex businesses, such as B2B2C companies.

Design Principles (or Product Principles)

Your design principles, or product principles, are a set of guiding beliefs and values that provide direction for your teams throughout product development, keeping them focused on what is truly important by guiding design decisions. Your design principles should illustrate the fundamentals that cannot be compromised without impacting the key customer outcome or maintaining competitive differentiation.

To understand the usefulness of design principles in action, consider the Swiss Army Knife. What makes it a great product? If you ask customers, most will mention the versatility of its numerous tools. While versatility is one of the Swiss Army Knife's most notable features, a standard toolbox is actually much more versatile than a Swiss Army Knife, providing many more (and better quality) tools.

No, what actually sets the Swiss Army Knife apart is its ergonomics: it's lightweight, it fits in your pocket, and it's relatively safe to use. Imagine you're the product manager for the Swiss Army Knife, and you decide to conduct customer research by watching some of your customers setting up a campsite. As you watch, you take notes about all of the possible improvements you could make to your product.

"Oh, the customers are cutting some logs with a handsaw. We should add a saw that can cut logs to the Swiss Army Knife. Oh, now they're using a compass to figure out where the sun will rise. Of course! We should include a compass."

In this way, you could just keep adding more and more gadgets to the product. After all, wouldn't you help the customer achieve more outcomes by making it *even more* versatile? This seems like a good idea, but it's actually a dangerous trap for a product manager. They would be breaking their design principles: a Swiss Army Knife that is two feet wide and weighs fifteen pounds no longer fits in the customer's pocket and would be horribly clumsy and unsafe to use. The relative value of the Swiss Army Knife would disappear and suddenly, the toolbox would start to look like the better product, even though the new Swiss Army Knife had more gadgets. This mistaken product direction is easy to recognize and avoid with physical goods, but in the world of software, without having explicitly defined design principles, it can go unnoticed for years.

In fact, this is a nearly ubiquitous problem for digital products. Companies just keep adding features based on customer requests or perceived gaps in functionality, but eventually, the product goes off the rails. All of the benefits of features they've added are outweighed by the collective damage they do to the customer's experience, especially during the trial phase. If the product team had put some clear design principles in place as part of their customer journey vision, many of these harmful additions would never have been made. Your design principles create the constraints governing your product decisions so you never lose sight of qualities that are vital to the customer journey.

Ben's Story

SETTING MEANINGFUL
DESIGN PRINCIPLES

At the energy-efficiency startup Opower, a question that was constantly asked throughout product development was, "How well are we adhering to the design principles we defined at the outset?" If we weren't doing so well in one category or had taken a step backward in another, we would prioritize an initiative to more closely match the principles we'd laid out.

Some companies develop design principles that are so generic that they may as well not be written at all, like, "Make the product easy to use." This doesn't help to drive decision-making, and in fact, it gives people license to take the product in many different directions at the same time because everyone has their own interpretation of what will make the product easy to use.

By contrast, Opower's design principles were always based around the unique qualities of the customer experience we aimed to achieve. For example, one of the design principles in our document was, "Assume people don't care." Research had revealed that consumers spend about nine minutes a year thinking about their energy usage, so how could we drive behavior change when consumers thought about the relevant issue so little?

That design principle drove us to create a product that would get the attention of that tiny sliver of their minds dedicated to energy usage, which was particularly important for us as a B2B2C company. If we couldn't *make* consumers care about their energy usage, our product would never have been successful at delivering the collective energy savings to the utility companies who were paying for the product. We made sure everyone in the organization knew this design principle and took it into consideration.

Another design principle was, "Always lead with action." The company was essentially an exercise in applied behavioral science, so we always had to think about how to drive people to change their behavior—by changing thermostat settings, turning off the lights more often, and so on. It wasn't enough, then, to simply tell a customer, "You use 10 percent more energy than your neighbors." We also included energy-saving tips in every report so customers could implement context-relevant changes.

Ultimately, through the exercises in this chapter, you are expressing your vision in a customer-centric way by showing what you want the customer journey to look like at a future point in order to deliver a 10x outcome. Once you've crafted your vision, visualized it, and refined it, it's time to create your strategic plan for realizing it. We'll look at how you do that in the next chapter.

ACTION CHECKLIST AND RESOURCES

Visit *buildwhatmattersbook.com* for an action checklist and resources such as templates, examples, and worksheets for creating your customer journey vision.

CHAPTER FIVE

PRODUCT STRATEGY

"Plans are worthless, but planning is everything."
—Dwight Eisenhower

n chapter three, you set your key customer outcome, which helped you measure product success from a customer's perspective. Then, in chapter four, you envisioned every step of the customer journey to achieve a 10x outcome. Now, it's time to figure out how to realize that vision.

Consider the European theater during World War II. Was there an end-state vision for the Allies? Absolutely. To march on Berlin, overthrow Hitler, and force an unconditional surrender. To achieve this vision, the Allies put together a complex set of steps that included:

1. Keeping pressure on the eastern front while amassing an army in the United Kingdom
2. Crossing the English Channel and establishing a presence in mainland Europe for a ground war on the western front

3. Establishing manufacturing superiority to advance the lines, forcing Germany into an unwinnable fight on multiple fronts

4. Converging on Berlin and ending Nazi rule

Were adjustments made to this plan along the way as the war unfolded? Of course. However, strategic planning provided a clear direction to reach the goal. In reality, the Allies *started* with the desired end-state—overthrowing Hitler—and worked backward from there to figure out a path to realizing it.

The WWII European Theater

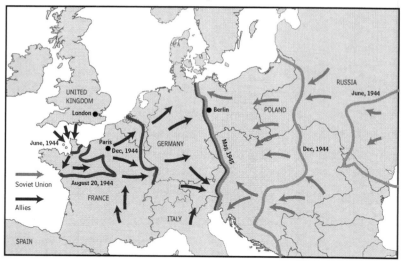

"If we want to overthrow Hitler, we have to take Berlin. If we want to take Berlin, we have to march our forces there. If we want to march our forces there, we'll need to win on the ground. To gain a ground presence, we'll have to establish a foothold on continental Europe. To land that army, we will need to first amass it in the United Kingdom. To support that army, we'll need to increase production and ration supplies."

For each step, logistical decisions had to be made. How will troops be moved? How will they be fed? How will they be armed? If they had skipped any of the steps or failed to consider dependencies, there's a good chance they would have lost the war.

The logic and dynamics are obviously important when fighting a war. Although business isn't war, the method for developing, executing, and adjusting strategy to achieve an outcome is very much the same. Now let's get back to business.

HOW WILL YOU GET WHERE YOU'RE GOING?

A strategic plan is about getting from Point A (where you are today) to Point B (your end-state vision of the customer experience). By itself, a vision doesn't mean much. You could envision anything, but without a formulated, practical plan to achieve it, your vision is just a fantasy.

If you wanted to climb to the summit of Mount Everest, you wouldn't just start walking uphill and hope to somehow find your way there. If you were coaching a team heading to the Super Bowl, you wouldn't show up without a game plan.

There is a perception in the Agile product community today that, because you can't perfectly predict the future, planning must therefore be a waste of time. We strongly disagree. Sure, moving in the wrong direction just because you thought it was the right direction initially would be a serious mistake, but having a plan, even one that is subject to change is far superior to having no plan at all. A strategic plan ensures your ongoing efforts are purposeful, and dynamically adjusting those plans ensures they remain so. It's okay to change your strategy along the way. In fact, it's essential.

Climbers who tackle Mt. Everest reconsider their timing based on the most recent weather forecast. Super Bowl coaches don't hesitate to make halftime adjustments based on what's working on the field. It's a best practice to consider likely scenarios, plan contingencies, and create buffers to make space for the unpredictable inevitabilities you'll discover through continuous validation work, which we will describe later in the book.

Dan Olsen, author of *The Lean Product Playbook*, explained it well, "The process of creating a successful product is necessarily iterative. Any strategy for achieving product-market fit includes many hypotheses that need to be tested along the way. As you test your hypotheses and learn, you will change your hypotheses and your strategy. That's not a sign you are doing something wrong; it's a sign you are doing it right."

WORKING BACKWARD

We believe product strategy definition is best done by *working backward* from the end-state vision rather than working forward from your current product. It's like solving a maze in reverse. You start with Point B, then determine all of the twists and turns that lead back to Point A, where you are today. You can also think of it as crossing a river by foot—as you stand on the bank, you look for a series of stepping stones that you can use as a path to get safely across the water. You wouldn't just step forward onto any stone without first evaluating whether it leads to a dead end.

The Path to Realizing a Vision

STRATEGIC PLAN
How you'll get from where you are to where you are going

Case Study

WHOOP: EXERCISING GREAT JUDGMENT

WHOOP was an advisory client for years prior to Ben joining the company as chief product officer in 2020. Founded in late 2011, the company produces a higher-end wearable device and mobile app for tracking overall health. Will Ahmed, founder and CEO, had a unique customer-focused vision based on a paper he wrote while he was a student at Harvard University titled "The Feedback Tool: Measuring Intensity, Recovery, and Sleep." His thesis was that properly understanding any one of these physiological statuses requires measuring all of them. Thus, heart rate and other metrics need to be tracked continuously.

In the early days, WHOOP had several technical challenges to overcome. How do you craft a device comfortable enough to wear 24/7? How do you accurately capture microfluctuations in heart rate, which is a critical factor in recovery? How do you charge a device without removing it from your wrist? Faced with daunting hurdles and complexity, outside experts recommended WHOOP use data from other instruments instead, such as chest straps, which at the time offered greater precision but were uncomfortable to wear. Rather than pivot to what was easier, the team pressed on and ultimately built the best on-wrist heart rate tracking device available.

According to Will, "Staying very committed to that initial vision was the key to our success. If you want to introduce something to the market that's truly novel or 'breakthrough,' you need to have a strong point of view, which may even feel contrary to popular conjecture. I always remind our team of this. We want to have conviction about what the world should look like for our customers when the product is being used successfully."

In other situations, though, WHOOP correctly pivoted based on market feedback. For instance, the high costs of the precision instrumentation embedded in the device made the product too expensive for consumers. WHOOP responded by switching to a monthly subscription model, resulting in much higher demand and an enviable growth rate.

How did WHOOP know when to remain steadfast and when to pivot? Referring back to the customer-focused vision was the key to making these difficult judgment calls. The company was willing and able to flex to match consumer preferences; how and when customers paid for the product was never an important part of the customer journey. In contrast, abandoning their own hardware investments would have necessitated pulling data from third-party devices, none of which were designed for continuous wear. Doing so would have broken the connection between sleep, recovery, and strain, which is foundational to the superior customer experience Will imagined when he founded the company.

Of course, choosing how to respond to market feedback or observed product usage isn't strictly binary. The WHOOP customer journey vision also included collecting user input about daily behaviors and then showing users how their behaviors affected their body, but the initial in-app questionnaires had low adoption. While it was tempting to remove the feature and invest in other parts of the experience instead, the team knew to dig deeper by conducting user interviews. They learned that many customers found the questions immaterial, so the product team replaced the static questionnaire with a new feature called "WHOOP Journal," which allows users to choose the questions they find most personally relevant. Adoption skyrocketed, and now WHOOP is uniquely able to report back to users how their behaviors (such as drinking alcohol) and circumstances (such as being sick) affect their performance.

Will said it better than we could. "If you don't listen to your customers, you're going to miss the important feedback you need to make a great product, but if you listen to customers too bluntly, you may lose sight of what the purpose of your product actually is." Being able to separate the two illustrates the value of producing—and committing to—a rock-solid customer journey vision.

GAP ANALYSIS

The first step in building a product strategy is to conduct a *gap analysis*, comparing your customer journey vision to what the customer's actual journey looks like today. This will require you to be brutally honest and unbiased in your assessment of how your customers interact with your product. The gap analysis reveals which key improvements or accomplishments are needed to realize the customer journey vision and deliver the 10x outcome. Gaps could include many things, such as product capabilities, data assets, user volume, brand awareness, partnerships or relationships, and more.

SEQUENCING THE WORK

Once you've done a gap analysis, you'll have a good sense of the magnitude of the task at hand. It can't all be done at once, so you'll need to sequence your activities. Take stock of the limitations and realities of your business, and identify and address any dependencies that exist, whether logical, technical, competitive, financial, or otherwise.

There are a few specific strategy drivers that you need to be aware of as you map your path from Point A to Point B and sequence your activities. Factors influencing your strategy include real-world business constraints, technology accomplishments, and dependencies or jumping-off points that can propel you to the next stage. The list of considerations can be long and complex for most companies. However, in our work advising dozens of companies on product strategy, there are a few that seem to come up time and time again:

Product Strategy Factors

 Navigating the Financial Situation and Fundraising

 Serializing Outcome Delivery

 Acquiring and Extending a Competitive Advantage

 Resolving Technology and Data Dependencies

 Serializing Market Segments

 Creating Strategic Leverage

Let's look at each of them in turn.

Factor #1: Navigating the Financial Situation and Fundraising

If your financial situation means you can't afford to build the things you say you're going to build without running out of money along the way, then your path to Point B will have to include securing additional funding or becoming cash flow positive first. Suppose you're a startup with only nine months of funding. You can't set a "pie in the sky" vision that will take twenty-four months to realize unless you are building what's needed to get an investor to fund the additional development. It doesn't matter how good your plan was if you cannot fund its development.

Set strategic milestones that investors will want to see to ensure you get the funding you need or set milestones to achieve profitability by providing sufficient customer value before you run out of cash. The key here is to know what you are up against, and ideally to prioritize development work that accomplishes both: appeals to the next round of investors (usually by showing traction) *and* makes meaningful strides in the direction you want to go.

Factor #2: Acquiring and Extending a Competitive Advantage

How can you acquire a competitive advantage, or extend the competitive advantage you already have? For this, we go back to the Kano Model, which we discussed in chapter four. Recall that the Kano Model breaks down product features into specific categories: must-haves, performance features, and delighters. Now, we're going to reapply the Kano Model to make product strategy decisions.

MUST-HAVES: EARN THE RIGHT TO PLAY

When sequencing the work to get you to Point B, bear in mind that it won't do you any good to build a new performance feature or delighter until you've included all of the must-haves. Your must-haves earn you the *right to play*, so they have to be your starting point. If you're designing a car, you can create the most amazing intuitive touchscreen that gives riders access to a range of interesting features, but functioning brakes, windshield wipers, and seat belts, as boring as they are, must be included. Until you include them, anything else you add is pointless.

Another vital feature of any car—an absolute must-have—is the ability to drive long distances without the vehicle ceasing to function. Tesla faced a dilemma because their electric cars used an energy source that gas stations in the US didn't offer. Customers had to plug the car in at home. This made Tesla's vehicles geographically constrained. The Model S had a better price tag than similar luxury cars, superior driving performance, an elegant touchscreen interface, a quieter and more comfortable ride—it excelled in every category except one: range. Despite all of its relative strengths and differentiators, the initial limited range of the Model S hindered sales.

It was a constraint on the customer journey that prevented them from achieving their desired end-state vision. Developing a bigger battery wasn't enough—tweaking the vehicle's range from 250 miles per charge to 280 miles per change wasn't going to assuage consumers' concerns about buying an expensive car that couldn't feasibly be taken on a longer road trip. Tesla had to think outside the box to solve this problem, and they came up with a fairly radical solution. Tesla built a supercharger network that provided free and fast charging to Tesla owners in locations with multiple dining options along Interstate freeways.

People almost never drive their vehicles all the way across the country, but Tesla made it possible anyway to communicate to potential customers that they could if they wanted to. In doing so, they addressed the must-have requirement and eliminated the primary objection against buying the product. This important strategic decision led to the tremendous success of the Tesla Model S, which served as a launching pad for the next phase in their plan. Tesla was then able to "cross the chasm" [Geoffrey A. Moore] by developing the Model 3, which finally fulfilled the original end-state vision for their product of taking electric cars to the mass market.

PERFORMANCE FEATURES: EARN THE RIGHT TO WIN

Once you've earned the *right to play* by including all of your must-haves, you earn the *right to win* by including performance features. To do that, think about the customer segment you're going after and their key criteria for making purchasing decisions.

Distinct segments within your target market will have different evaluation criteria, or they may prioritize those criteria inconsistently. Where many companies stumble strategically is by going after a market that's so wide that building a product to serve all their needs proves an impossible task. It's fine to have ambitions to eventually expand. The trick is to find a segment of the target market for whom you can build a superior product when compared to *all* alternative solutions recognizing that the yardstick for that comparison will be the set of performance features that *that specific segment* cares about most.

DELIGHTERS: EARN THE RIGHT TO WIN AGAIN

You earn the right to win with your *performance features*, but it's your *delighters* that will really keep customers coming back. Although they are often overlooked, delighters add to the product's "coolness factor" which can help you win again and again by contributing to customer love and product evangelism. People enjoy talking to friends about (or showing off) these cool, unexpected features. We never recommend skipping delighters in a product strategy, and if the discovery stage of your customer journey vision includes word of mouth, they become essential.

Delighters are not just valuable for word-of-mouth marketing. They also contribute heavily to customer engagement and retention. While delighters are, by definition, unexpected at the time of evaluation and trial, customers can become so attached to them during their engagement phase that they couldn't bear to be without them later, so when some new product comes along that could potentially steal your customers away, they are inclined to disregard it. Delighters drive loyalty.

The best way to measure the impact of delighters is to approach customers who score the product as a perfect ten on a net promoter score (NPS) survey and ask what pushed the product all the way to ten. Chances are, they will mention the delighters that really wowed them.

PRIORITIZING DELIGHTERS IN THE MVP

Product managers and designers usually have a lot of good ideas for delighters they can include in their product, but they struggle to get executives to support prioritizing them. After all, the value of delighters tends to be hard to measure. With must-haves and performance features, there is almost always a clear ROI and value proposition, so delighters get pushed out, particularly when it comes to defining the minimum viable product (MVP).

Indeed, some people believe that a minimum viable product includes, by definition, only the must-haves. However, for any product—including an MVP—to succeed, it needs to include a combination of must-haves, performance features, and delighters. This is because delighters are critical for driving one of the most important metrics in your business: customer retention.

If you only include must-haves and performance features in your MVP, your users are less likely to come back for a second or third time, and you run the risk of drawing an incorrect conclusion that the market opportunity for the full-featured product isn't good enough. This mistake is referred to as a false negative, in which a product's lackluster response gets misinterpreted as evidence that the product doesn't deserve continued investment when, in fact, continued investment is exactly what would make it succeed.

Factor #3: Serializing Market Segments

You may start with one type of customer, then move on to another. For example, some companies start in one geographic market and then expand globally from there because the dynamics in the initial market make it easier to establish a foothold, and the learnings from that first market can be useful in later phases. Serialized market segmentation applies to expanding geographically, but can also be based on other market dimensions. Here are just a few examples.

- Vertical or sector (example: non-profit organizations → government → commercial)

- Customer size and sophistication (example: SMB →
  enterprise)
- Use case (example: wedding registry → baby registry)

Factor #4: Serializing Outcome Delivery

You may also consider delivering value related to the same overarching outcome for the same target market segment, but doing so in phases. A familiar example is a Costco membership. Originally, it only included the ability to shop in their warehouse stores. Over time, they added access to digital photo services, travel services, refinancing options, car sales, eye examinations, and more. They are targeting the same customers but increasing the value proposition by adding layer after layer of value.

More firmly in the technology space, consider similar examples:

- Beyond free delivery, Amazon Prime offers streaming content, discounts at Whole Foods, and unlimited photo storage.
- Beyond solo video game playing, Sony PlayStation offers social gaming and tournaments, streaming apps, Blu-ray movie playback, and audio services.
- Beyond spinning classes, Peloton offers scenic rides, yoga, mindfulness, and weightlifting content, and a mobile app.

By taking this approach, you are effectively creating new nodes in your customer outcome pyramid from chapter three to enhance your value proposition. Often, this means expanding from offering a single product to offering a multiproduct *platform*, which is a very common element of the longer-term visions we see from the startups we've worked with. You can also keep a single product and deliver against other outcomes for customers. Note that this approach requires establishing trust with the initial product. In all of the examples above, these companies delighted customers with their first product, which enabled them to get adoption for subsequent features and products.

Factor #5: Resolving Technology and Data Dependencies

Technology and data dependencies are those assets that are necessary to support your future customer journey vision.

People may not realize that LinkedIn actually makes most of their money through their paid recruiter tools, which enable users to find information about candidates or search through job listings. Most people think of LinkedIn as a professional social media platform, a place to make business connections, rather than a paid recruiter tool.

However, the social network was merely a necessary first product that laid the foundation for their real moneymaker by giving them the data capability they needed to power their paid recruiting tools. Now, recruiters can solicit more applications for their job openings and proactively search for candidates by skill and location, which provides a superior product for recruiters, which no one else can compete against because no competitor has LinkedIn's proprietary data set.

Making the up-front investment to create a proprietary data asset can be a powerful strategic move that can pay dividends later through smart product development, marketing, and monetization. Be aware, though, that it also usually takes a long time to establish and necessitates a strong initial funding position, or at least confidence in your ability to secure additional funding down the road.

Factor #6: Creating Strategic Leverage

Strategic levers are those things you can use to gain an advantage with your product, such as relationships, partnerships, patents, or other assets. When Apple first launched the iPhone, it had an exclusive deal with AT&T, which required early iPhone customers to have a contract with AT&T. That partnership drove a huge amount of business in both directions. If you were already an AT&T subscriber, Apple was clearly the top choice, and if you liked the iPhone, you had to become an AT&T customer. This made it quite difficult for other smartphone companies to compete and strip away business from Apple *or* AT&T.

When thinking about product strategy, don't constrain yourself to thinking only about technical, strategic levers like data, algorithms, and user-generated content. Nonproduct advantages, such as business relationships, well-known reference customers, thought leadership position, SEO dominance on particular keywords, and brand equity are also leverageable assets that should absolutely be considered in developing a product strategy. This is especially important when you are first to market as your early success will draw in new competitors, but your early traction gives you an edge you should exploit to maintain the number one spot in the new category you've created.

A great example of this comes from our shared operational experience at Opower, which was the first to market with a *behavioral* energy efficiency solution for utilities; all prior solutions were programs aimed at simply replacing inefficient physical products (lower-energy light bulbs, better windows, newer refrigerators, etc.). The sales team knew that any utility company under pressure to reduce energy waste was taking a bit of a gamble by spending millions of dollars on this new approach, which was all about getting consumers to change their habits. In a highly consultative sale, Opower's "money slide" was simple: a graph showing a consistent history of results driving down energy consumption for previous clients.

Regulated utilities were often mandated to issue an RFP from multiple vendors, ensuring Opower would face direct competition, but it won the vast majority of deals by recommending that utilities ask competitors to produce a similar slide. None of them had results yet because Opower was first to market with behavioral energy efficiency, and this sales approach absolutely kept it that way, allowing the company to dominate the market it established.

This story illustrates an important point—a robust customer journey vision should transcend product development and align *all teams* toward a common strategic plan.

Establishing Milestones

As you consider these factors to sequence the work and fill gaps on your way to a vision, think about the major milestones along the way, and how you'll know when it's time to move into the next strategic phase. Usually, a strategic plan can be boiled down to about three to five milestones, which are good indicators of progress and points to take a step back again before pressing forward. We suggest using your outcome pyramids to measure progress towards those milestones so that others—investors, employees, and perhaps even customers—can celebrate achieving a strategic milestone.

These milestones will serve as good places to *reassess* your strategic plan, natural points along the way to determine whether you need to make adjustments. Common reasons to change your strategic plan include rapid market changes from an economic shock or regulatory shift, newly identified technology hurdles, changes to the company's financial runway, and groundbreaking moves by competitors.

Arriving at milestones is often the right point to share updates with the CEO and executive team, including:

- Development accomplishments-to-date
- Results and learnings so far
- Next steps in the original strategic plan
- Adjustments to that plan you intend to make now or are considering

We find this to be a great structure for board meeting updates on product management.

PIECING IT ALL TOGETHER

Remember our fictional startup Chuckwagon? Their end-state customer vision was to help customers get a home-cooked meal without spending a lot of time. Their product strategy is based on serializing outcome delivery for the same target audience, traversing the consumer outcome pyramid by adding features to save time during meal planning, then grocery shopping, then cooking, monetizing each feature set along the way.

Chuckwagon: The 5-Year Plan

	Recipe Plans	Grocery Delivery	Home Chefs
WE ARE HERE	One tap to get a personalized recipe plan for the household for every meal this week.	Convert meal plans into grocery lists for one tap ordering.	Make it easy to get a chef to come prepare your week's meals for you.

	Milestone 1 (2020)	Milestone 2 (2022)	Milestone 3 (2024)
Business KPI	**$2M ARR** $2M monthly subs	**$10M ARR** $5.3M monthly subs $4.7M grocery orders	**$50M ARR** $36M monthly subs $10M grocery orders $4M home chefs
Customer KPI	Save time meal planning.	Save time grocery shopping.	Save time cooking & cleaning up.

VISION
Save Americans millions of hours in deciding what to cook, buying groceries, and preparing high-quality, home-cooked meals.

But why did this sequencing make sense as their product strategy? Chuckwagon knew they didn't want to build a grocery delivery business, but in order to integrate with the likes of Instacart and Shipt, they had to first show a sizable user base to make an integration interesting to those partners. Chuckwagon wanted to bootstrap their business and further show traction in Milestone 1 by demonstrating that their Recipe Plans saved so much time, consumers would be willing to pay for them. Similarly, they recognized that it would be operationally complex to have hundreds of chefs going to thousands of homes with specific ingredients to cook any meal under the sun. Once the meal plan was set and the groceries were in the house, it would be much easier to manage the logistics of having a chef come and make the food now that the list of recipes had been whittled down to a manageable number.

In this way, Chuckwagon's strategy depended on three of the factors we called out earlier: navigating the financial situation (by bootstrapping), serializing outcomes (saving time in three different steps of cooking), and strategic leverage (partnerships with Instacart and Shipt that would also drive users to their other revenue streams). Chuckwagon's strategic plan below shows how different company initiatives will deliver a customer journey across the different milestones they set. For example, the first milestone's customer journey starts with bloggers and influencers driving users to try the 1-Tap Meal Plan feature and eventually pay for it.

Chuckwagon Strategic Plan

	TRIGGER	DISCOVERY	EVALUATION	TRIAL	USAGE	RETENTION
Milestone 1	Bloggers/Influencers		5-Star Reviews	1-Tap Meal Plan		ID At-Risk
				Free ▶ Paid Conversions		
					Meal Ratings	
Milestone 2	NPS/Referral System				Grocery Lists	At-Risk Email
	Instacart/Shipt Partner Emails				Grocery Delivery	
Milestone 3	Invitation to Use Chuckwagon from Chefs				Book a Chef	

While the Chuckwagon product strategy may sound straightforward, we know that product strategy is really difficult. It's one thing to select an amazing 10x outcome and craft a compelling customer journey, but figuring out the steps to get there can be incredibly complex. Your strategy is going to be unique to your company and product, and, as we've shown, there are quite a few factors that will impact the path you choose to your desired outcome. Crafting an effective strategy is as much an art as a science.

To get it right, bring together the right people and spend sufficient time hashing it out. We will cover best practices for doing this in chapter seven. Keep in mind that your strategy may shift and evolve over time, and that's okay.

Of course, you won't be able to invest *all* of your resources into realizing your vision because you have other financial considerations in running your business. In the next chapter, we'll look at how you can create a roadmap that balances investment in your vision with all of the other product development work that keeps your business healthy and growing in the short- and medium-term, as well.

Case Study

DRFIRST: CLARIFYING THE DIRECTION FOR A NEW PRODUCT

Since 2000, DrFirst has pioneered healthcare technology solutions and consulting services that securely connect people at touchpoints of care to improve patient outcomes. DrFirst calls its product portfolio the "Healthiverse, an interconnected healthcare universe where information silos are shattered and where all stakeholders aspire to a higher purpose: improving patient care." Prodify started working with their consumer product managers in July 2019, a few months before they launched Huddle, a mobile app to keep medication and medical records organized. The product manager for Huddle, Valerie Garrison, saw how important a detailed vision and strategy are at product launch:

"When building a brand new product, it's easy to believe you're focused. For Huddle, DrFirst started out with a simple and intuitive vision of allowing consumers to collect, organize, and share health records. However, as new ideas and use cases popped up, it became increasingly difficult to explain why one idea fit into the vision for Huddle and another didn't. Prioritizing between many good ideas started to feel impossible. Several pieces of the Vision-Led Product Management framework helped us crystalize what we're really doing with Huddle—today and in the future. For one, starting with the top outcome for our users and breaking that down was the perfect foundation for everything that followed. It was a north star that we could always come back to. Then, mapping out a customer journey in detail helped us see which parts of the product journey we had figured out, and which parts needed improvement. Each step of the process built off another part, which created a cohesive connection from the vision to the roadmap."

One of the key areas we worked on with Valerie was prioritizing the target audience and use cases. Was it for new parents, so they could feel on top of things by tracking doctor appointments and immunizations? Was it for siblings who just started taking care of their elderly mom and needed to share notes after each visit on how she's doing? In answering these questions to decide where to focus, we also considered factors such as the frequency of the use case, the urgency of getting records organized, and the satisfaction with existing solutions (especially paper filing). Once we decided on the target audience, the right set of key performance indicators (KPIs) wasn't crystal clear. Most consumer products use metrics like monthly active users, but is that appropriate for episodic use cases like a child's annual vaccines?

While we can't share all the details of what Valerie decided with Huddle, she was finally able to present to executives and other stakeholders a concrete story on the product's success metrics and how the near-term roadmap for Huddle connected to a longer-term vision for the product as a part of the DrFirst Healthiverse ecosystem. In particular, the presentation allowed Valerie to proactively answer stakeholder questions like, "When can we scale this product?" by laying out the path to helping millions of Americans better manage their own health and that of loved ones.

"Working through the frameworks and defining all of these important pieces of our product wasn't easy. It took hours of thought, required input from stakeholders and users, and plenty of rework as our thoughts matured. However, having the framework was essential. I've been in situations before where we wanted to define these things, but no matter how much effort we put into it, we couldn't. The Vision-Led Product Management framework made the difference with Huddle."

ACTION CHECKLIST AND RESOURCES

Visit *buildwhatmattersbook.com* for an action checklist and resources to help you think through your strategy, explore the factors discussed in this chapter, and see more product strategy examples.

PART

III

BRINGING VISION-LED PRODUCT MANAGEMENT TO YOUR COMPANY

CHAPTER SIX

CREATING A BALANCED ROADMAP

"Everything in moderation, including moderation."

—Oscar Wilde

B y now, you have established the "power train" of product leadership by identifying your key customer outcome, crafting your product vision, and creating a strategy for getting there. However, unless you're a startup launching the company's first product, you have to show a plan for how to execute on that strategy while balancing the needs of your existing product's customers, along with everything that comes with sustaining your business.

WHY ROADMAPS ARE VALUABLE

Before we get into creating a roadmap to balance all the needs simultaneously, we wanted to emphasize why we think roadmaps are necessary given some recent debates within the product management community on the value of a roadmap:

1. A roadmap connects the near-term product changes to the mid-term strategic milestones and the long-term vision.

2. At a product-driven company, a roadmap helps other teams like marketing and sales plan their initiatives based on the direction of the product. You can think of the roadmap as the grease between the product gear connected to the motor and the other teams whose gears turn in concert with the product gear.

3. A roadmap communicates the sequencing of priorities and helps spark discussions to create alignment around those priorities.

4. A roadmap facilitates communication about top-level priorities between the product leader and individual product managers on the team.

THREE CATEGORIES OF PRODUCT DEVELOPMENT

Based on our experience, we've realized that all product development activities can be placed into one of three categories: innovation, iteration, and operation. Let's look briefly at what they are.

1. **Innovation:** Making progress against strategic milestones towards the vision.

2. **Iteration**: Getting better results from what you've already built, including minor improvements, new features and one-off requests, A/B tests, and other optimization.

3. **Operation**: Maintaining your product and running your business, including technical architecture, performance, security, bug fixes, and uptime. This category can be thought of as revenue protection.

3 Categories for Roadmap Balancing

1	INNOVATION	Bold changes to make leaps and bounds towards the customer journey vision	EXAMPLES • New features • Overhauls to existing features • Architectural changes to support a future end state • Integrations with partners
2	ITERATION	Incremental changes to the existing product to deliver additional customer & business value	EXAMPLES • Conversion funnel optimizations • A/B testing • Small fixes that provide incremental lift of a KPI • One-off feature requests or enhancements
3	OPERATION	The cost of managing a modern SaaS product	EXAMPLES • Security / data privacy • Performance / uptime • Technical debt / upgrades • Internal tooling • Bug fixes

Each of these categories represent three workstreams that should be happening simultaneously, but how do you know the ratio of time and resources to spend in each? In reality, you will allocate your time and resources differently depending on where your product is in its lifecycle.

WHY YOU SHOULD
ALLOCATE TOP-DOWN FIRST

We recommend starting by making a top-down allocation decision, saying, for example, "We want to put 60 percent of our investment toward innovation, 30 percent toward iteration, and 10 percent toward operation." This kind of top-down allocation carries a multitude of benefits.

First, it ensures that executives understand the trade-offs that have to be made. This forces a discussion up front about what the intentional allocation should be between innovation, iteration, and operation before getting into the weeds. Too often, companies skip this step and end up with some allocation percentages across these categories not by design but by accident as a side-effect of the individual smaller-scale feature prioritization decisions. This should be obvious, but big decisions need to come before small ones.

Second, it helps to ensure that the right decisions are made for the company and for the customer. Often, the disjointed (or ulterior) motives of competing stakeholders with varying degrees of influence in the organization can have an outsized pull on roadmap priorities. This constrains the level of influence any particular stakeholder can have by ensuring balance before any lobbying efforts for individual product improvements begin.

Third, top-down allocation helps to prevent a situation where product managers are constantly playing defense while stakeholders are clamoring for more time and resources for their relative priorities. When the product leader takes the time to get every team aligned to a top-down balanced roadmap, they provide the necessary air cover for product managers to push back against the litany of demands and one-off requests that would otherwise overemphasize short-term iterative improvements at the expense of innovation and operations categories. The opportunity cost of saying yes to one-off requests is remarkably high. Recall that a hallmark of product-driven companies is to be able to say *no*, and a top-down allocation is very helpful in creating space for saying *no*.

Fourth, it prevents product managers from having to take on an impossible task of comparing apples to oranges to grapes, which is exactly what they're doing when they have to compare roadmap items across all three categories. As we will discuss later, each category has its own appropriate prioritization methodology, which makes comparisons across categories particularly challenging. With a top-down allocation in place, apples only get compared to apples, which in turn helps to avoid the "business school" dysfunctional pattern from chapter one, where a company sinks into analysis paralysis for every tiny prioritization decision.

An ancillary benefit is that it can address the sometimes antagonistic relationships and politics that engulf product management, allowing you to make allocation decisions from a position that is above the fray. Instead of having individual teams clamoring for resources, top-down allocation provides an overarching framework that aligns every team to common goals centered around the customer and the long-term growth potential of the company.

In the book, *Product Roadmaps Relaunched*, Product Culture founder Bruce McCarthy makes a strong case for a clear prioritization framework as a defense against the chaos of reactivity. "I've seen it turn quarreling executives into an enthusiastically aligned team in short order. The key is to agree on the desired outcomes before attempting to prioritize anything, and then to work your laundry list through that framework together as a team."

All of this contributes to the health and well-being of your company culture. We will talk about your culture in much greater depth in the last chapter of this book.

Ben's Story
THE TOKENS SYSTEM

Earlier in the book, I told the story of Opower's color-coded roadmap, which highlighted the inconvenient truth that our willingness to say yes to inbound feature requests from RFPs was perpetually pushing out our more innovative and strategically valuable work. This is the story of how we finally broke the cycle.

Every B2B SaaS company dreams of being able to build a product, make it available to customers, and have them buy it and get value from it without having to do any customization or product additions to close new business. With excellent product management and salesmanship, that is achievable within most industries. When selling to regulated utilities, on the other hand, it is not. No matter how robust the product capabilities, there will always be some idiosyncratic customer need that has to be accommodated. To have a hard and fast rule of saying no to all feature requests would have cost Opower almost every single deal we won. In effect, we were selling a square peg to fit a differently shaped round hole each time, and the peg had to be modified slightly, or it just wouldn't fit. That burden fell on product development.

The difficulty was in making the right decisions about when to say yes to a feature request because it was a modification that was needed and when to say no because the deal could still be won without it. Enterprises are notorious for putting "the kitchen sink" into their RFPs in hopes of getting vendors to solve a slew of problems outside of the original scope. If I had been an Opower salesperson, I would have pushed for us to say *yes* to every single request in the RFP to maximize the chances of winning a deal, and that's exactly what the sales-people at Opower did.

Of course, in my role running product management, I wanted to say *no* to every feature request because saying yes meant further pushing out roadmap priorities. It was a stalemate, and while everyone appreciated that we were on the same team, it created an antagonistic relationship and a zero-sum game between sales and product. Something had to be done.

Dan Yates, co-founder and CEO of Opower, called the VP of sales and me into his office to work it out. We asked ourselves the question, "Forgetting about the specific feature requests and roadmap priorities on the table today, what percentage of our development capacity is appropriate for saying yes to win deals and what percentage should be reserved for true product development?" It was a simple question, and to my amazement, all three of us agreed immediately: given the realities of the market we were selling into, about 15 to 20 percent should be earmarked for client commitments and the other 80 to 85 percent should be reserved for the roadmap. All we needed to do then was come up with a process for prioritizing the right work while holding ourselves accountable for matching the top-down allocation we had just set.

And so the tokens system was born. As long as sales could operate within their capacity allocation, I didn't feel strongly about what we actually prioritized as long as it resulted in us hitting our sales targets. Sales was in the best position to determine which items were worth committing to and which could be ignored. It worked much like a paid time-off plan in which for every few weeks an employee works, they earn days that they can take for vacation. As long as you remain within your earned vacation time, the company has little say in when or where you go. In the tokens system, for every eighty-five developer-days of product roadmap work, we would add fifteen developer-days of capacity or "tokens" to a budget that sales could use as they deemed necessary. (I did have veto rights for requests that would result in scalability issues or overwhelming product complexity, but I rarely had to use that power.)

This process was controversial, particularly within the engineering team, who felt product management should never defer to other teams. It was controversial enough, in fact, that it has become a classic case study taught at Harvard Business School. Regardless of how people felt about it, the results spoke for themselves:

1. A junior salesperson working on a small deal couldn't come to the product team directly, banging their fist on the table about a pile of feature requests. They had to instead go to the VP of sales, who would shrug the request off immediately, noting that unless the deal size were larger, it wouldn't be worth using up their limited tokens. Eighty percent of the one-off requests that used to come to product management vanished overnight.

2. When the estimate for a truly important feature request came back higher than the salesperson expected, rather than try to force it anyway, they asked us whether we could work with them (and when possible, the client) on an 80/20 solution that would solve the utility's need but at a fraction of the token expense. This is exactly the kind of constructive discussion we had always wanted.

3. If several different clients were asking for additional product features that were roughly the same, sales leadership would ask whether they needed to spend tokens multiple times. I would respond by explaining that they didn't need to spend them *at all*. Enhancing the product to satisfy the evolving needs of the market is exactly what we intended to do with the remaining 85 percent of the roadmap anyway. This was precisely the type of market insight we were looking for from our client-facing teams.

DETERMINING YOUR ALLOCATION

The right allocation across three categories of innovation, iteration, and operation depends on several factors, but mostly the stage of your product. Keep in mind that if you have multiple products, you might have a different allocation for each one. We've provided our general thoughts on the appropriate percent allocation for a product based on its stage in the table below. Of course, the allocation toward each category of investment will depend on the corporate objectives, the competitive landscape, and more, so you should adjust accordingly.

Roadmap Balancing by Product Lifecycle Stage: Rules of Thumb

Lifecycle Phase	Innovation	Iteration	Operation	Focus Area
Pre-Alpha/Idea	100%	0%	0%	Bringing vision to life with alpha release
Post-Alpha/ Launch	30%	60%	10%	Addressing alpha customer feedback, although might still be innovating towards vision
Beta/Circling Product-Market Fit (PMF)	10%	70%	20%	Iterating rapidly to find PMF
General Availability/ Scaling after PMF	10%	20%	70%	Scaling product to support the internal operational needs that arise from explosive customer/ user growth

Lifecycle Phase	Innovation	Iteration	Operation	Focus Area
Steady State/ Maintaining	60%	10%	30%	Looking ahead at next wave of innovation/ strategic milestone

In the earliest stage, when your product is little more than an idea that you're just beginning to code, there are no existing customers. You have no product to operate, so your focus is 100 percent in the innovation category. However, once you release the first version of your product, you'll almost certainly go through the painful experience of realizing you got many things wrong. This is totally normal, to be expected, and simply part of the process. Now, it's time to begin talking to early customers to get feedback and spend a lot of time improving upon your product.

You're not ready to grow and scale a business around it yet, but you have a product out there. Perhaps 60 percent of your time and resources shift from the innovation category to the iteration category. You still don't put much in the operation category, other than bug fixes, because you have a limited number of customers and scaling won't be a priority for some time.

Once you get close to product-market fit, having implemented tweaks based on feedback and your product needs to be ready to scale rapidly, your focus should shift from iteration to operation. As you add more customers, experience growth, and hire more team members, you also start to implement various internal tools to manage customer service and maintain the operational side of the product.

Eventually, you reach a steady state, where you're primarily doing maintenance. You're still probably spending about 10 percent of your time on iteration, but the product is mostly stable. You've found product-market fit. Perhaps 30 percent of your time now goes to maintaining and operating the product, which leaves more capacity again for innovation. After all, you need to start thinking about what strategic milestone comes next, whether that's the next generation of the same product, a new module or extension, a product in an adjacent space, or expansion into a more grand vision, such as a multiproduct platform.

A PRIORITIZATION FRAMEWORK FOR EACH CATEGORY

After making a top-down allocation decision, you'll need to prioritize within each category as well. A different prioritization framework is needed for each individual category. In other words, you will prioritize your *innovations* differently than you prioritize *iterations* or *operations*.

Innovation

For innovations, think about the strategic milestones you have to reach to realize your product vision. This is Vision-Led Product Management in action. What things do you need to prioritize in order to get to the next milestone? After all, if you skip a critical milestone, you probably won't achieve your end-state customer journey vision. Clarify the tasks you need to complete to get to the next milestone and set goals for your team to deliver them.

By focusing intensely on delivering against the milestones you identified in your product strategy, you avoid falling into the trap of being overly responsive or aimlessly making "improvements" without actually innovating. Your strategic plan will prove very helpful at this point, though you probably need to delve into a greater level of detail now as you implement it.

As was the case with authoring the customer journey vision and strategic plan, product management needs to partner with engineering leadership very closely when planning the innovation priorities for the product roadmap. This allows them to understand the long-term roadmap direction and strategic milestones so they can appropriately design the system to support them. In our experience, technical debt is not as much an issue of rushed development, as is usually cited, but more an issue with product management not being clear about the future needs of the product early enough with engineering. Pulling engineering leadership in at this critical stage can help to dramatically reduce technical debt down the road.

Providing this forward-looking view to engineering allows them to make smart decisions about what technical debt is actually important to pay down, where rewrites of the code base are necessary, and where new modules, services, or systems infrastructure need to be crafted. By working with engineering collaboratively and engaging leadership in the strategic product direction, product management:

- Builds trust with engineering leadership
- Generates buy-in and excitement for the direction of the product

- Allows for smart technical decisions that will avoid the creation of new technical debt
- Improves the long-term scalability and extensibility of the product
- Shrinks total development time by preventing work on unstable, complex, or antiquated parts of the code base that are inefficient to build upon and really do need to be refactored

Prioritization within the innovation category also requires paying close attention to where you are in the *S-curve of innovation*. The S-curve of innovation, first used by sociologist Gabriel Tarde in 1903 and later popularized by communication theorist Everett Rogers in 1957, is a common visual for depicting the way in which businesses derive value from innovation over time. It's rarely a straight line.

The S Curves of Innovation

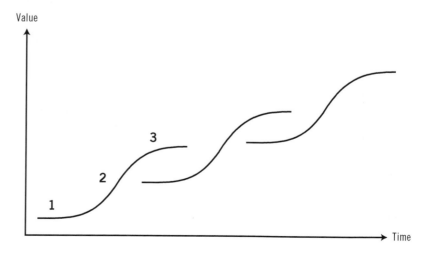

1. In the beginning, plenty of work goes in, but little value comes out until the product is robust enough to create real customer value for a big enough market. When it does, the product has achieved product-market fit. This is the first stage in the graphic above.

2. After that, with relatively little additional investment, the product can scale quickly and create massive value for the business based on the value it delivers to customers. This is the second stage in the graphic above.

3. Eventually, continued innovation yields diminishing marginal returns as customer expectations evolve and the weight of the product makes further innovation more challenging. This is the third stage in the graphic above.

There is always the danger of your current product reaching a growth plateau, and while A/B testing for optimizations is both good and necessary, it will not create meaningful growth in a product that has reached its limit.

That growth flatline is a critical time in the product's lifecycle. That's the place where lackadaisical VPs of product get fired, where customers get bored, and where disruptive competitors will pull the rug out from under you. Innovation takes a long time to deliver results in the beginning stages of a new product, so if you're well into the plateau of your legacy product before you start thinking of your next innovation, you're too late.

You'll need to make a judgment call about when the right time is to continue innovating on your existing product and when the right time is to shift gears to start innovating on a new product or module altogether. A key factor to monitor is whether the value you're delivering to customers is slowing down. Other factors include market conditions, customer stickiness, "moats" you've created to protect your business, the product's revenue impact, and customer sentiment. There's no magic spreadsheet to calculate the right moment to make this switch. It's a very tough judgment call that justifies why the senior-most product executives get paid the big bucks.

Iteration

For the iteration category, your focus becomes incremental value delivery: to the customer, to the business, or to both. What improvements can you make to deliver more value to customers with your existing product? How can you make your existing products perform better? Iteration includes things like new or improved features, funnel optimizations via A/B tests, user experience enhancements, and so on. Unlike the other categories of innovation and operation, where priority decisions are amongst a few big important options, the iteration category typically has a multitude of initiatives with different purposes and benefits and ranging in scope and level of effort (LOE) from tiny to huge. This is where a much more scalable (and slightly more quantitative) approach is needed.

"RICE" is a simple but robust prioritization framework developed by the team at Intercom that many product managers use. It stands for *Reach, Impact, Confidence,* and *Effort,* and it can be especially helpful in the iteration category for determining which initiatives to prioritize. RICE provides a scoring system based on the four factors in its name. Essentially, you evaluate a project in terms of reach, impact, and confidence, then divide the result by the amount of effort it will take. Scoring can be done using whatever scale works best for you, such as 0 through 10, or t-shirt sizes (extra small, small, medium, large, and extra-large). The end result is the RICE score for your project. The higher the score, the greater the priority.

- **Reach**: The number of customers/prospects you expect to reach.
- **Impact**: The magnitude of the business result you anticipate for the affected customers.
- **Confidence**: The degree of confidence your team has that you will actually see the results you expect.
- **Effort**: The resource allocation required to complete the project over a given period of time, typically measured in "story points" or "developer-days."

To arrive at your RICE score, use the following formula:

RICE Prioritization Formula

$$\frac{\text{Reach} \times \text{Impact} \times \text{Confidence}}{\text{Effort}} = \text{RICE SCORE}$$

Often, our clients are confused when it comes to measuring confidence. What is the difference between being 70 percent confident or 80 percent confident? It's not always so clear, so we recommend you triangulate on confidence from different information sources:

- **Quantitative data,** such as click-through funnels or a segmented engagement analysis
- **Qualitative data,** such as usability testing results or insights from sales calls
- **Competitive intelligence,** such as seeing a must-have feature doing well in another app

Let's suppose you need users to click through five steps to complete a registration form, but your data indicates that most people are only clicking through the first four and dropping off before finishing. What can you do to get them to click on that final button?

You start by conducting user interviews to hear users explain why they are unable or unwilling to finish. You use A/B testing, trying variations addressing the feedback from the user interviews until you find a change that encourages the users in the test group to complete the final step. You might also look at successful competitors, or perhaps companies outside your space who are known to do this well, to see how they are getting customers to click through similar flows. In doing so, you are combining competitive intel, qualitative research, and quantitative analysis to increase your level of confidence in making a change that you wouldn't be willing to prioritize otherwise based on the confidence component of the RICE model.

When we discussed this with Holly Hester-Reilly, Founder of H2R Product Science and host of *The Product Science Podcast*, she explained more broadly, "More and more people are practicing continuous discovery and experimentation, but I still often see people doing research without thinking enough first about what they want to learn. I always encourage people to think critically about the research itself. Be intentional about how you can design experiments to get the information you need to de-risk your development activities as cheaply and quickly as possible. When you take the time to go through these steps in your customer research, the impact of that research will be much higher."

The RICE model can be a very useful starting point. It can clarify that a feature everyone thought was a good idea simply doesn't have the reach to justify being a development priority. It can also identify small initiatives with high impact that might have otherwise been overlooked. However, we never recommend taking the output from the RICE model at face value and blindly setting priorities accordingly. Too often, the set of priorities are just a collection of unrelated quick wins that users are unlikely to even notice. It's *always* worth reviewing the output and doing some post-processing.

Questions to ask about the set of priorities:

- Looking across the priorities generated, does it seem as though there was any bias built into our scoring?
- Do the priorities generated align with our beliefs about where product investments would be most valuable? (For example, if you already knew that the product was feature-heavy and the RICE model's output was a bunch of additional features, perhaps you should remove some of them and sprinkle in UX cleanup work to reduce cognitive overload for new users.)

- By swapping a few items that are above and below the prioritization cut line, could we group work into more cohesive themes?
- What are the implications of this set of priorities for stakeholder groups? As examples, will this force customer success/support to have challenging conversations with customers? Will marketing have enough to discuss at the upcoming user conference? These may not be the primary reasons to prioritize one feature over another, but they are valid considerations when evaluating the output.

Operation

For the operation category, your focus becomes the ongoing maintenance of your existing products and the cost of running them. Typically, this includes a number of distinct considerations, such as:

- Service-level agreements (SLAs), such as 99.999 percent uptime or page load times being under a threshold of 1.5 seconds
- Data privacy requirements, such as HIPAA compliance or GDPR compliance
- Security requirements, such as 64-bit encryption at rest and two-factor authentication
- Cost of goods sold (COGS—an accounting measure of the cost to run the product), such as AWS hosting expenses
- Other operating expenses and challenges, like conducting regression tests and pulling data out of production into a data warehouse for internal metrics reporting

Of course, security is an ongoing concern, especially when company or customer data is involved. One of our clients uses an internal rating system of silver, gold, and platinum for their platform security, ranks initiatives based on specific security factors, and then strives to get to a platinum rating.

Prioritizing these types of product improvements against customer-facing product improvements and longer-term innovation is nearly impossible as there's no basis for comparison; it's difficult to assign a dollar value or customer value to a single bug fix, but too many of them will certainly frustrate customers and turn them away. That's why we feel it's better to reserve a percent of product development for the operation category and allow stack ranking of nonfunctional requirements, security holes, technical debt, bugs, and the like against other initiatives in the same category.

Many of the clients we work with know they need to do operational work—fixing bugs, conducting maintenance, and resolving technical debt—but they aren't sure how often to do it or when. If they allocate 25 percent of their investment toward operational work, does that mean putting 25 percent of every sprint toward operations, or does it mean doing operations work exclusively every fourth sprint? Should they create four different teams and assign one to do operations work all the time, so the other teams don't have to worry about it?

All of these are viable ways of approaching operations work, and some teams prefer one method over another. You can also make ad-hoc, game-time decisions along the way and then reassess your allocation percentage each quarter. If you've made a top-down allocation of 25 percent but then find during reassessment that you only spent 15 percent of your investment in operations, you can ratchet it up during the next quarter. If you hit above your allocation, you can bring it down.

In regard to fixing bugs, you can adopt a zero-tolerance policy, where you fix them as soon as you find them, or you can set a service-level agreement (SLA) that specifies how long a bug is allowed to remain in production before it needs to be fixed, which can vary depending on the severity of the bug. Note that in the same way you might say no to some requests, some bugs might be so minor that you mark them as "will not fix" to close the loop. No product is perfect.

A third way of handling bugs is to set a quality score for production with a maximum threshold for the number of bugs that are allowed to be in production at a given time, broken down by severity. For example, maybe you're only allowed to have two "top priority" bugs in the system at any given time, but 200 small-scale defects. As you approach those thresholds, you know it's time to do more bug-fixing work. This final method of handling bugs is the one we typically recommend because it allows a product leader to actively manage the quality of their production code. If you place a cap on the number of defects that are allowed, you can shift that limit up or down depending on the relative importance of quality versus the emphasis placed on new feature development.

Regardless of which operational or bug prioritization framework you choose, make sure it's documented and that there's alignment so stakeholders understand how this work will be handled.

Rajesh's Story
THE BUSINESS VALUE OF OPERATIONAL TOOLS

When I was on Ben's product team at Opower, my goal was to increase our margins as we prepared for the IPO. My squad was called "SaaSy Ops," a nod to the fact that we wanted to drive down the personnel costs of operating our product so we got the same valuation multiples as other SaaS businesses when we went public. We did this by automating tasks that our product operations team had to do manually because the product didn't support them.

One of the manual tasks we automated was the selection of energy-saving tips shown on the back of Home Energy Reports. I spent my first month or two just observing how the team curated these tips using complex logic and a set of spreadsheets that were manually loaded into the database right before millions of Home Energy Reports were generated each month. It took hours for a team of three or four energy efficiency marketing experts to do this every few weeks—time they could have spent on other work to encourage energy efficiency at home.

In the end, our squad collaborated with our internal users and built what we called Automated Tip Targeting (ATT) to automatically choose personalized tips for every report. We codified a lot of the rules the tips team had informally been using and built a feature toggle to turn on ATT by client.

We thought we were done after training the tips team on how ATT worked and how to enable it, but the tips team wanted to be sure that ATT would choose the right tips for the right user given a specific set of conditions (e.g. which tips would go to a user with electric heat in Boston in October). We built a feature to project which tips would be chosen for a given user type over time. The result? The tips team felt much more comfortable turning on the feature, and that drove adoption.

For me, the key lesson was that building operational tools for internal stakeholders should be approached like you would building a product for a customer or external user.

ACTION CHECKLIST AND RESOURCES

Visit *buildwhatmattersbook.com* for an action checklist and resources to help you with top-down allocation of investment across the three categories, prioritization scorecard templates within those categories, and roadmap templates.

CHAPTER SEVEN

THE RIGHT PROCESSES

"There's a way to do it better. Find it."

—Thomas Edison

We've discussed selecting your key outcomes, creating your customer journey vision, crafting your strategy, and creating a balanced roadmap. Now, we want to provide some specific, actionable steps you can take to implement each part of Vision-Led Product Management at your company, from planning and strategizing to getting alignment and communicating important decisions to your teams. Then we will explore some processes for maintaining your Vision-Led Product Management artifacts. First, however, let's examine specific tactical steps for identifying your key customer outcome.

STEPS FOR IDENTIFYING THE
KEY CUSTOMER OUTCOME

We recommend bringing your executives together and letting them each take a stab at identifying what they think the key customer outcome is. Ask everyone to imagine your customers—pull up personas or customer research insights to get everyone into the right mindset. Now, ask them to write down what they think the customers' most common answers would be to the question, "How do you know if this product is delivering value to you?" You'll likely be surprised at the answers you get—they might be all over the place. Consider each of the answers you hear to be hypotheses, which can all be tested.

The best way to get alignment when there are differing perspectives is to collect data by conducting customer research. When speaking with customers, we recommend using *The 5 Whys*, a technique developed by Taiichi Ohno at Toyota back in the 1950s. The idea is to ask a series of five "why" questions consecutively to arrive at a customer's real need—sometimes called "root-cause analysis." Applying this approach to determine a customer outcome, you could imagine the following interaction:

"Why did you buy the product?"
I really liked the feature that auto-tags and indexes our files.

"Why is the file tagging feature important to you?"
Because it's hard for the patent lawyers to find the files they need otherwise.

"Why do they have trouble finding the files they need?"
Each "prior art" researcher uses different naming conventions
for the files they save, so there's no way for a patent lawyer to
be totally sure they haven't missed something.

*"Why is it so important for a patent lawyer to see every single
relevant file?"*
Because if they miss one, then the client's patent application
could be rejected.

*"Why would a rejected patent application be such a big prob-
lem for you?"*
Our firm prides itself on our high patent application acceptance rate; it's what we advertise and guarantee to our clients.
Any rejection puts the entire account at risk, which could
potentially cost us millions.

Eureka! Asking "why" five times gets from a *mundane* statement
like, "I really liked the auto-tagging feature," to a valuable and
actionable (and potentially lucrative) outcome statement like,
"What I really need is risk mitigation, and solving that is worth
a ton of money to me." Not bad for a short bit of work.

Where possible, use a combination of *quantitative* and *qualitative* data, which we talked about in the previous chapter to
arrive at a key customer outcome that your leaders can agree
on. Remember to use customer research to predict what prospects in the pipeline will want as well as future market trends.
You don't want to solve a problem that isn't going to exist by the
time your product hits the market.

We've seen a lot of teams struggle when it comes to identifying their key customer outcome metric, and if that's you, here are some tips on getting to alignment:

1. **Identify the decision-maker.** Typically, this is the product executive, or another executive if the product executive hasn't been hired yet.

2. **Call out different customer segments/personas.** Identify key outcomes for each one separately as they often vary and prioritize the segments/personas against each other later when you create your product strategy.

3. **Document the decision.** The decision-maker should write down the assumptions made, the options considered, and some rationale for why the key outcome was chosen for reference purposes down the line. Trust us, "Why did we choose this key outcome?" will come up as a question later.

Once you've chosen your key customer outcome, put it down on paper or somewhere official, then make sure you have alignment between the founder/CEO and executives before you proceed to the next steps of the process, or your vision may be optimizing for the wrong outcome. Create outcome pyramids from both the customer's and company's perspectives by breaking the key outcome down like a math equation, or into "pillars of value delivery." The metrics at the bottom of the pyramid should measure product usage, meaning they can change rapidly with every release. The value of this is that the product usage metrics aren't random or isolated—you can visualize how they ladder up to the delivery of a key customer outcome, and they are likely leading indicators of success.

If you do need to change a key outcome of the customer or business outcome pyramid, hold a special meeting to explain why, how it will affect in-flight work and any impacts of the change on the product vision, strategy, and roadmap. This way, the team has a chance to understand and discuss the change and how it affects them.

STEPS FOR CRAFTING THE CUSTOMER JOURNEY VISION

Now, you're ready to begin crafting your customer journey vision, which will clarify what experience will yield a 10x outcome. To get directional feedback on your vision, we encourage you to talk with forward-thinking customers who seem to have a good sense of where the market is headed. They can help you understand if the key customer outcome you've selected is the right one, and they can also provide feedback about whether the customer journey is inspiring, realistic, and valuable, which will help you in the next step of the process.

External validation before internal validation keeps your internal discussions from devolving into a debate over the opinions of your highest paid or most influential team members. Sadly, this is a part of the process that often gets overlooked. Product teams get so bogged down with their own processes that they forget to spend time on customer discovery. Make sure to carve out sufficient time for speaking with customers to hear their reactions and identify potential holes that, if not addressed, could sink your entire vision. The cost of not doing so is just too high.

Don't forget to also get direct input from:

1. Your **customer-facing teams.** Include sales, marketing, customer support, and account management, because they can provide additional guidance and a unique perspective as you construct the customer journey.
2. **Engineering leadership.** Engineering needs to verify the complexity, technology risks, and feasibility of delivering the customer journey vision within the time horizon, given assumptions about resource allocation and team growth.
3. **Third-party sources.** Explore reviews and community content found in the App Store, included in influencer blog posts, industry reports, or on review sites, such as Capterra.

Asynchronous Iteration

Using all of this information, carve out time for yourself to craft the customer journey, including the six major stages: trigger, discovery, evaluation, trial, engagement, and retention. Write this down in a short format, calling attention to any major assumptions or known validations. Use any (or all) of the visual communication tools that we recommended in chapter four, including comic strips, visual mock-ups, and customer diary entries.

While we suggest starting with ideas from the entire executive team for choosing the key customer outcome because the debate is healthy and the variety of hypotheses are useful for conducting customer research, we actually recommend taking the *opposite* approach for crafting the associated customer journey vision. Instead, go heads-down for a while and draft something, and once an early version is available, begin sharing it with stakeholders one at a time. Allow them to react to it and be willing to make wholesale revisions based on the feedback you collect. This may seem inefficient, but consider what the alternative looks like. Everyone would be sharing their own independent ideas for what the ideal customer experience should be, and each contributor outside the product team would be blind to some critical pieces of the puzzle, such as technology limitations, business model impact, and so on. Having everyone start from scratch in parallel would be a clear case of having too many cooks in the kitchen.

As it solidifies, share your customer journey vision with your product team, with customers, and with prospects in your current and future target market to obtain feedback which you can use to further refine or redirect the vision. Once you've made adjustments, rinse and repeat until you've addressed all relevant feedback, closed all gaps, and strengthened any weak areas. Keep in mind that you need to get *commitment*, but 100 percent *consensus* is likely a pipe dream. In fact, if you do get complete consensus without meaningful friction, you should consider it a warning sign that you aren't being bold enough or that the executive team is exhibiting "group think."

STEPS FOR CRAFTING THE PRODUCT STRATEGY

Once you have alignment around the key customer outcome and the customer journey vision, it's time to craft your product strategy for getting there. In our experience, it's most effective to work on your strategy together cross-functionally and to do that, we recommend conducting an offsite strategy meeting that includes your product, design, engineering, marketing, sales, and customer success teams. Before starting, you need to make sure your vision is clear because it's going to be hard to strategize if there's vagueness about what you're working toward or the constraints you need to respect.

Pre-Work

Before meeting with your teams to strategize, set the proper context by sharing any customer research you've conducted in advance. This ensures that you will be dealing with the realities in the market and not merely spouting opinions.

When you invite your teams to your offsite strategy meeting, make sure you ask them to come up with some ideas beforehand. Encourage everyone to be prepared to share and provide feedback—this should be more of a discussion than a presentation. You don't want one person dominating the meeting. When everyone shares, the commonalities and disconnects become clear, so you can address them.

Resolving the Disconnects

During this process, you will probably discover that stakeholders have different ideas or incompatible beliefs about the best path to take in realizing the product vision. Identify the disconnects and break them down to understand the root point of disagreement. Is it a difference in risk tolerance or a preferred mitigation plan? Is there a disagreement on whether a competitive threat needs to be handled? Are there different beliefs about the direction the market is heading? Is it something that can be resolved with a simple survey sent to existing customers? Once the big disconnects are identified, either make the difficult decision and address the feedback or lay out a plan for collecting more data or pulling other people in to help decide.

It's often more important to get agreement on the decision-making *process* than on the decision itself. Remind collaborators that the strategy is a living document, it's not set in stone. You will continue to learn as you go and will have ample opportunity to make adjustments later. Even some of the most successful technology companies have made major strategic errors along the way. They were successful anyway because they were willing to observe, learn, apply, and adjust.

You can't please everyone, and you can't embrace every individual's ideas. Ultimately, the decision-maker should be the CEO, or the product leader if they are empowered as such. Stakeholders should be treated as advisors and contributors, but they don't get a *vote*. Product strategy is not best determined democratically. If you can't get everyone on the same page, then you're going to have to make some tough and perhaps unpopular decisions to move forward. That's part of the job of the product executive. As Jeff Bezos says, "Disagree and commit."

Offsite Session

When it's time for your strategy session, you may be tempted to use a large conference room at your office, but we prefer using an offsite meeting location because it gets your people outside of their normal, everyday environment. This, in turn, helps to create space for creativity and bold thinking, and a neutral location reinforces your culture and sense of teamwork. If you're able to meet in person, select a location with plenty of wall space and bring lots of Post-It notes so you can put ideas, thoughts, and facts on the walls as they come up. If you're working remotely, as is the case for many companies responding to COVID-19, ask the team to join from a location that isn't their normal office to get them into a different mindset, something that feels different from the day-to-day routine. Use an electronic whiteboard or other real-time collaborative tools like Google Docs, along with the features like Zoom breakout rooms to emulate in-person activities.

The product leader, such as the chief product officer (CPO) or VP of product, or the CEO should guide the conversation, but encourage everyone to participate in the discussion, because every team member needs to feel invested in the strategy. Some companies find it helpful to use an outside facilitator to level the playing field, so team members aren't intimidated or reticent to offer their ideas. Give the meeting plenty of time—perhaps a full day with a break for lunch—so you don't rush the conversation.

Avoid falling into the trap of "kicking the can down the road" when you reach one of these difficult decisions. Try to deal with it then and there even if some of your team members can't agree, especially for decisions affecting engineering priorities leading to the next milestone. Call out any assumptions, risks, or pivot points that you observe or identify any next steps to help you get alignment with everyone.

Be sure to identify your key success milestones, as well as reassessment milestones along the way. This is going to be a long meeting, so take generous breaks from time to time to help your people reenergize and refocus.

SHARING THE OUTCOMES, VISION, AND STRATEGY

By this point, you should have created your key customer outcomes, your product vision (including every stage of the customer journey), and a strategy for realizing that vision. Once all of these are ready, it's now time to communicate them to your entire company. This is your chance to shine as a product leader because your ability to get everyone aligned will largely depend on *how well* you communicate, not just what you communicate. Be prepared to address any questions or concerns that come up by predicting what you might hear in advance.

We can't say this strongly enough—your presentation quality matters tremendously. We recommend rehearsing your presentation before you share the outcome, vision, and strategy with your company. Have some of your in-the-know team members pretend to be inexperienced employees so they can listen to your practice presentation and predict some of the more challenging questions you might get.

If you don't communicate a coherent story or seem to not be fully bought-in yourself, people will be less likely to believe in you as a visionary leader. On the other hand, if you do it right, people are going to get excited about the vision, about your leadership, and about the opportunity in front of the company as a whole. A well-presented vision and strategy ripples throughout a company in an amazing way, so practice well and get feedback from trusted peers. Refine your presentation, choose your words well, craft helpful visuals, and make it compelling. Don't just stand up there and talk—*inspire* people to think about the product from the customer's point of view.

At the same time, let people know that your vision and strategy are living documents that will require reassessment and readjustment along the way. "We'll continue to learn as we go," you might say, "but this is where we are headed currently." Build in the expectation of flexibility, so people don't assume you expect them to follow every step blindly. Communicate the milestones as points where reassessments are already planned, but most importantly, get them excited about the end-state customer vision.

Ben's Story

LETTING CUSTOMERS SPEAK

One of my most important responsibilities at GoCanvas was being the author and steward of the product vision and strategy. After I had worked to get executive alignment, it was time to present the package to the whole company. The team had done a great deal of customer discovery, quantitative research, stakeholder interviews, and more, but there was still a risk that employees who were unaware of those efforts might think we were operating out of an ivory tower. Rather than bore them with a long preamble about our process, I decided to let the customers simply speak for themselves.

One of our research activities was recording interviews with customers, including both those that we won and those that we lost. I went through all of those interviews and cut audio highlights for each. Then I spliced them together into "chapters," so we could hear our customers *and noncustomers* tell us what they were looking for at each stage of their journey, points at which they felt engaged, and areas where we fell flat. I edited intentionally but honestly so that even quotes that countered my point of view were included.

Instead of presenting slides, I just played five-minute audio segments where multiple customers explained their key outcomes, what they wanted in an ideal customer journey, and gaps in the GoCanvas product experience—all in their own words. All I did was take notes on a whiteboard and summarize after each chapter.

At the end, I took a photo of the whiteboard and then shared a pre-written document that mirrored the whiteboard notes. This became part one of a three-part series of presentations I gave at GoCanvas to generate enthusiasm for our product vision and strategy, and it built enormous trust in product management from all corners of the company.

ADJUSTING DIRECTION

Now that you've crafted your outcome, vision, and strategy, and you've communicated all of this effectively to your entire organization, you need a process for keeping your Vision-Led Product Management documents up to date. How frequently do you need to reassess, and who should be involved in those decisions?

Ongoing Validation

First and foremost, you need to build a discipline of ongoing discovery and validation, which will come from talking to customers regularly. You should always be learning from customers and the broader market, both directly and indirectly through customer-facing teams.

Continually test the assumptions that are embedded into your vision and strategy as you make progress against both. You may find that some of your assumptions were wrong, in which case, you can adjust accordingly.

Most companies don't do enough customer research. Though customer research should drive what they build, it is woefully underemphasized and underfunded, and since they don't have a dedicated person conducting research, the product managers or designers are expected to do it themselves. However, since research is then everyone's third or fourth priority, it doesn't get much attention.

At best, they might simply conduct some usability studies and assume they're doing a decent job. They'll build a prototype and invite customers to use the product, then ask them probing questions, observe where users struggle and make design changes accordingly.

The problem with this approach is that it is largely reactive. Customer research is only being used to deal with problems for an initiative that's already been prioritized, but it's not informing the decision-making about what to build in the first place. The thinking goes something like this:

"Let's design a product, build a prototype, then test it with customers to make sure it's not terrible. We'll fix any problems we encounter and put it into production."

But what if the initiative itself is actually the wrong thing to work on? What's the point of optimizing a product that doesn't meet a customer or business need?

In reality, a company needs to embrace customer research at every stage of product development, including the initial decision-making about what goes into the pipeline. A robust customer research practice should include a large chunk of the following: primary and secondary market research, persona development, card-sorting studies, diary studies, a customer advisory board, win/loss analysis, surveys and interviews, and, yes, usability studies. Once you have a team of about four or five product managers, you should strongly consider hiring a specialist focused exclusively on customer research so that it is always a priority.

If you don't have a specialist focused on customer research, we recommend spending at least four hours per week doing some form of customer research. While four hours might seem like a lot, keep in mind it's only 10 percent of a person's week, which seems reasonable for ensuring that you're building what matters for your customers. Still, if you can't commit that much right away, think of how you can build up to it over three or four quarters.

Case Study

MARKETSMART: CONSISTENT USER RESEARCH

In late 2017, Elizabeth Weiland heard Ben's *This is Product Management* podcast episode on mentorship and reached out to Prodify to find a mentor as she stepped in to become the first product manager at MarketSmart. MarketSmart's products are designed to help fundraising gift officers at nonprofits land more meetings with major and legacy donors, whose donations play a huge part in helping a nonprofit achieve its mission.

Like any startup PM, Elizabeth had to make tough prioritization decisions, so we used the Vision-Led Product Management framework to help her make those choices. We discussed different ways to connect with customers and users to inform the product direction. One of the first things we did together to better understand what key outcome customers sought was to run a one-time importance versus satisfaction survey to see how customers prioritized different outcomes and how satisfied they were with their existing solutions to achieve those outcomes.

The results from this survey prompted some new questions that no survey could realistically answer, so Elizabeth set out to conduct user interviews to better understand how customers viewed the value of her product and where they wished it did more. The survey results and user research summary served as a preread for a one-day vision and strategy workshop with the executive team, which helped the team identify a pathway to hitting their next business milestone by delivering new value to customers.

As Elizabeth reflected on the engagement and how it shaped the future of the product, here were her three key takeaways:

- "**Create a product vision**. We *still* use the same product vision and mission in describing our dashboard (though this will be expanding to encompass our entire product suite). Understanding the importance of the vision of our dashboard has given us a north star and ensured that we do not stray from that. It's been instrumental in setting OKRs on a quarterly basis. Before having a product vision, we were building features based on a gut feeling instead of listening to what our customers wanted and needed.

- **Talk. To. Your. Customers**. You hear it everywhere, but for whatever reason, it can get pushed back, and then you hesitate to pick it back up. When my work piled up, I stopped talking to customers for a few months. But I lost sight of what customers wanted... what their pains were...what they thought we were doing really well. Getting back into interviews even if there's not a topic (for instance, just a check-in to see how things are going and see where the conversation takes us) is *crucial* in my role, and I'm now passing on the best practices I learned to our UX researcher/designer. When you don't talk to your customers, you lose sight of what matters to them and can fall into the trap of building the wrong product or feature and wasting your time, engineering's time, and possibly losing a customer!

- **Consider different types of research to better understand your customers**. Yes, learning how to structure user interviews is important. Surveys can be insightful, but the one thing that truly helped lead us down the path to our next major revenue goal that we refer to constantly is the result of the importance versus satisfaction survey, particularly for donors and fundraisers. The outcomes of these surveys have been a constant reminder of what donors and fundraisers actually want, and where they feel there is a gap. It especially continues to make the product team keep donors at the forefront of everything we do. 'How will this make the donor feel?' The results have sparked ideas about how we can create new products nonprofits can purchase that will satisfy the fundraiser wants *and* the donor wants."

Ongoing Iteration

In addition to doing customer research to validate your direction, you also want to track your outcome metrics to ensure the product changes in the iteration category are delivering incremental value to both customers and the business. This quantitative feedback loop to measure actual customer/user behavior is an important part of making data-driven decisions to inform your product vision and strategy.

Case Study

OCTOPUS:
RAPID EXPERIMENTATION

Octopus Interactive is a rideshare media company based in Washington, DC. Co-founder and COO Brad Sayler explains the history of the company and an early product feedback issue they encountered their first few years:

"Most of our team members started our product careers with a lifestyle app called Spotluck that helped consumers decide where to eat and save money at restaurants. This app was fairly involved, so it relied on consumers to adapt and learn it over time. The feedback loop was long – anywhere from thirty to sixty days depending on the complexity of the new feature we'd introduced. To further confound our analysis, the product wasn't intended to be used every day or even every week, so when usage varied, we had difficulty attributing it to product changes versus seasonality versus folks simply forgetting to use it. Thus, we had no reliable measurement to gauge user adoption/satisfaction."

Prodify began working with Brad and his product team during the pivot from Spotluck to Octopus, and Brad knew they would finally have a short feedback loop they could use to inform product iterations. As he put it, "For our next product, we transitioned to a simpler, briefer experience—a micro-experience, wherein we installed entertainment/advertising screens in the back of rideshare vehicles. No app download required, no need to be front-of-mind, simply look up and tap the screen if you'd like to interact. We only have a few minutes to capture someone's attention, but this micro-experience provides us a rapid, strong feedback loop."

But what was the right metric to use to know if this tablet was working? Octopus had an interesting choice to make, as their product served *many* stakeholders who all sought different outcomes:

- Brands and their agencies who wanted to build awareness, drive traffic, or collect leads
- Drivers who wanted to provide a better rider experience to increase tips and ratings
- Riders who wanted a change of pace from staring out the window or at their phone

In the end, Octopus chose a product metric that has stood the test of time as a stable indicator of value for all stakeholders. In Brad's words, "By measuring content interactions per driver hour, we can quickly see if a new feature boosts user engagement. This quantitative measurement gives us nearly real-time accurate feedback—results on day one of a new feature are similar to results on day thirty or sixty." The beauty of the "content interactions per driver hour" metric is that it was a simple, durable metric that encompassed the outcomes sought by every Octopus stakeholder:

- Brands want to know how many riders are engaging with their content and how often
- Drivers want to offer riders an engaging experience (normalizing by "driver hour" allows Octopus to track the *rate* of engagement over time, even if driver hours fluctuate)
- Riders want to engage with the tablet if it looks "interesting" (note that the definition of an interaction could change over time—in response to COVID-19, the Octopus team tested Trivia Party, a way to play their most popular trivia game from your own phone as a way to engage with the tablet *without touching the screen*)

With this metric in mind, Octopus built their product team and operations around optimizing it. They created operational tools that let product designers and product managers create new games and ads for riders without involving engineering. They split *every* city into two cohorts of drivers so they could run A/B tests over the same time period and know the city wouldn't influence experiment results. They used "content interactions per driver hour" to monitor if and how engagement changed when they integrated with ad tech markets to fill their ad capacity. As Brad concluded, "Our rapid feedback loop, combined with a reliable measurement technique, allows us to continually iterate and optimize our product with phased roll-outs (and roll-backs when needed) and A/B testing."

Making Updates

We recommend reassessing both your roadmap and vision at either the one-third or one-quarter mark of your overall time horizon. So, if you have a one-year roadmap, you should update it quarterly. If it's shorter, then you should update it even more frequently, so that you never find yourself with too little visibility into your future plans. If you have a three-year vision, you probably want to update it at least annually.

Any time you review your vision or achieve a strategic milestone, take some time to reassess your strategy and make sure you're still on the right path. You may discover a better path to the next milestone, so be willing to make adjustments accordingly. You might even discover that there's a different milestone that you need to be working toward instead.

Be cognizant of other major market changes that may necessitate a strategic pivot *between* milestones, such as a competitor launching a cheaper, better product than yours or new regulations that immediately change the demand curve. The bottom line is you don't want to be operating on a strategy you know is no longer correct just because it had been correct once upon a time.

Handling Inbound Product Requests

There will always be more inbound product requests than the team knows what to do with, and these could come from customers, support, sales, the engineering team, partners, the CEO, or any other stakeholder, and you need a process for handling and responding to all of these inbound requests. Often, product managers try to cobble together all of these desired changes and requests, playing *product management Tetris* so they don't have to say *no* to anyone. But by finding a way to say yes to everyone, they are effectively saying no to the most important yet silent party, the customer.

Case Study

ORDERGROOVE:
REFRAMING THE QUESTION

We've worked with Paul Fredrich for many years across multiple companies. He is currently head of product at Ordergroove, an omnichannel commerce platform that makes subscription purchases and reordering easy. The company has effectively created a new category, which they refer to as "relationship commerce." While exciting, it has yielded an interesting challenge for Paul at the same time. The abundance of feature ideas, problems to solve, and potential strategic opportunities require him to be highly selective about what to invest in with limited development resources. Although ruthless prioritization is an important function of the *head of product*, there's a risk of him being perceived by stakeholders as the "head of saying no to good ideas."

One of the ways we've mentored Paul is in communicating *why* good ideas sometimes don't make it onto the roadmap. After some iterative process improvements, these are the approaches Paul is now using to ensure understanding and appreciation of the difficult trade-offs that he needs to make:

- Maintain an "idea bank" for product suggestions, including those that are not on the roadmap. Everyone has visibility into it and is encouraged to contribute their ideas, and all ideas are welcome.
- Provide transparency not only about what's on the roadmap, but what's not able to make it onto the roadmap and why. The underlying constraints and rationale are always communicated along with the roadmap contents.
- Establish a simple, consistent framework to assess each idea's impact versus effort—in this case, RICE—to compare product initiatives fairly. All

parties understand the framework being used for comparison.

- Regularly review the ideas in the "idea bank," their respective RICE scores, and corresponding ranking. The team takes the time to share these back with the stakeholders who submitted the ideas to avoid surprises when the roadmap is presented later.

For Ordergroove, the issue has rarely been *whether* an idea has a solid business case when evaluated in isolation. The core question needed to be reframed as, "Is this idea *so much better than* all the other good ideas that it's worth displacing them?" By implementing these approaches, Paul has successfully shifted the company's mindset resulting in far more confidence in its product roadmap and prioritization process.

Getting input on your roadmap along the way is very important, but how it's done matters. Don't just ask stakeholders what they want and try to jam all of the requests into the roadmap. When talking to sales, of course they are going to be driven by immediate sales targets. Generally, when they make a product request, their thinking is, "I need to add this specific new feature so I can close this specific deal." However, the only requests that should be included on the roadmap are those that contribute to the end-state vision for the product or will help to close additional new business down the road because the customer's demand is, in fact, representative of broader market demand.

Here are a few points to keep in mind when collecting stakeholder input on product priorities:

- They won't understand the trade-offs or consequences of their feature requests.
- They don't have an awareness of the opportunity costs involved.
- It's not their job to understand either of these. It's the product manager's job to listen and then account for them.

As a tactical matter, here are some sample questions you can ask different internal teams as you formulate your roadmap. The innovation questions are intended to encourage bold, long-term thinking. The iteration questions are intended to solicit ideas for extracting incremental business and customer value from the existing product. Finally, the operation questions are intended to tease out the unique perspectives each team has on the operations of the product and business.

You may notice that a lot of questions below ask the stakeholders for a "top 1-2" list. This is a form of "outsourced prioritization." Rather than ask for a laundry list of ideas or requests, ask *them* to stack-rank their ideas against each other so you don't have to. Just make sure you find out *why* they prioritized them at the top of their list as their prioritization rationale provides great insight into how they think of the value the product can deliver.

Sample Roadmap Input Questions to Ask Stakeholders

Stakeholder	Innovation	Iteration	Operation
Founder(s)/ CEO	Do you still agree with our vision and strategic milestones, based on market trends?	Are there any modest tweaks to our current product that you think would unlock outsized customer or business value in the near term?	Do you have any concerns about the technical stability/ scalability of our product?
Finance	What time horizon is allowable to show investors the impact of product development?	What parts of business operations are most important to drive efficiency for?	How much should we focus on growth versus profitability?
Sales	What 1-2 areas do you think we could better serve customers that would result in explosive sales growth in the next 2-3 years?	What 1-2 small fixes could we make to the current product that would help close more deals in the next 1-2 quarters?	What are the top 1-2 operational concerns from prospects? (provide examples like uptime, time-to-launch, security)
Marketing	What are the top 1-2 market trends you're seeing that we need to address in the next 2-3 years?	What 1-2 small improvements could we make to the current product that would help grow the pipeline in the next 1-2 quarters?	What tasks are taking up your time that could be automated?

Stakeholder	Innovation	Iteration	Operation
Customer Success	What 1-2 key outcomes do you think we should help existing customers with over the next 2-3 years?	What 1-2 small fixes could we make to the current product that would encourage trial, usage and retention in the next 1-2 quarters?	When speaking with customers, what information could be made available to you or them that would make you more effective or productive?
Engineering	What 1-2 key technical opportunities do you see as groundbreaking in terms of delivering on customer and business outcomes over the next 2-3 years?	What are 1-2 incremental technical/UX changes you think we could make to improve key performance indicators (KPIs) in the next 1-2 quarters?	What are the top 1-2 pieces of tech debt/ infrastructure you think we need to address? How should we measure technical quality/stability/ scalability?
Design	What are the 1-2 areas where you think we can deliver 10x results on key outcomes for customers in the next 2-3 years?	What are the 1-2 biggest design issues you think we need to solve with the current product in the next 1-2 quarters?	Are there technical constraints that could be lifted to make you more productive working with engineering?

Now that you have all of these questions answered, you have to figure out the best way to prioritize them against each other. When developing business cases for roadmap initiatives, the numbers have to make sense, but it's a poor use of time to conduct a net present value (NPV) analysis for every project unless it's launching a completely new product or hiring a new team to develop it. Most of the time, common sense is enough, and it's certainly a hell of a lot faster. Don't lose sight of the big picture, which is a far greater risk than failing to optimize financial returns down to the penny.

Ensuring Roadmap Balance

Your roadmap can be a useful tool for pushing decisions down through the product management organization. It creates a handoff point for the product leader, so they don't have to pay attention to every detail of every individual sprint. As long as the team of product managers commits to the roadmap, and there is sufficient buffer in the roadmap to accommodate small-scale twists and turns, then the product managers can be empowered to make whatever decisions they need to, as long as they stay on track delivering the roadmap priorities.

If they get off track, or they learn something that makes them want to reconsider the roadmap priorities, then it automatically sparks the need for a discussion between the product manager and the product leader so that the right decision can be made and everyone remains on the same page about what's being worked on and why. By using a roadmap to delegate responsibilities to other team members, a product leader can regain some of their time, focus, and sanity. Furthermore, delegating decision-making authority below the roadmap level is necessary for scaling a product organization beyond just a handful of people.

When balancing your roadmap among the three categories—innovation, iteration, and operation—track each of your features or user stories and tag which category they belong to. That way, you can go back periodically and make sure you are balancing your investment appropriately. You don't have to be a stickler about this—but capture enough information so you can make sure your allocation percentage in each category is roughly where you want it to be. If your allocation is off, you can easily spot it and make adjustments accordingly.

EXECUTING YOUR ROADMAP

Everything has been leading to this point. You have top-down allocation, you've created a process for maintaining your vision documents and deliverables, and you have a process for keeping the roadmap up to date. Now you have to communicate and deliver the items on that roadmap.

You've probably seen some version of the ever-popular Agile/ Scrum process diagram, but have you ever noticed that there's usually a huge missing piece in the process? They typically tell you to start with your perfectly prioritized rank-ordered product backlog and from there, plan your sprints and continue the process of software development. All of that is well and good, but there's just one problem. Where is this prioritized product backlog supposed to come from? Is it just supposed to magically appear?

The simple answer is no—your product backlog doesn't magically appear; you have to build it. For all the books, articles, and blog posts available on Agile development practices, there is remarkably little content available about determining what should go into the backlog in the first place, yet product managers have to make tough choices *on a daily basis* to manage the prioritized list of user stories and other tasks the team will work on next, which is where the rubber finally meets the road.

The Magical Backlog

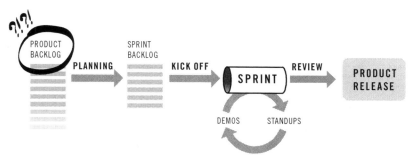

We've already talked about the three categories of investment—innovation, iteration, and operation—but it's important to note that each category gets filled using a different set of methodologies. You use your vision and strategic planning to feed the innovation category, while customer feedback, new features, and A/B testing feed the iteration category, and bugs, internal tools, and other technical improvements feed the operation category. Collectively, these items get merged into the product backlog, where they are then chopped up into sprint backlogs through a collaborative session with engineering (for teams using Scrum) and ultimately into product releases.

Using Roadmap Buckets to Create Sprint Backlogs

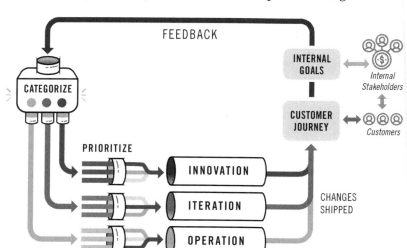

One of the unintended consequences many teams face in moving to Agile/Scrum methodologies is that in an attempt to build iteratively and ensure all work fits into short sprints, they end up prioritizing only small, bite-sized product improvements in the backlog. These user stories are less likely to advance toward realizing a longer-term vision. That's not to say they're not worth pursuing, but this is why there are different categories for innovation, iteration (where these stories fall), and operation. Interlacing the rank-order priorities for each of the three categories based on the top-down allocation bucks this trend and forces more innovative work into the backlog. These initiatives will still need to be fragmented into small-scale user stories with incremental user or business value, but because they are in the innovation category, you can have confidence that those stories aggregate into larger epics that collectively reach strategic milestones.

Creating the Roadmap Document

Many leaders are confused about what goes into a roadmap, so don't worry if you're one of them. There is no right answer: different types of roadmaps suit different companies. We've seen them printed on ten-feet-wide poster paper, as a simple Google Sheet or Trello board, or embedded in a specialized software tool specifically for roadmap management and presentation. They can appear as Gantt charts or as lists; they can show lots of detail or very little; they can be intentionally scrappy or highly organized with color-coding, iconography, team associations, and more. While there is no "best way of making a roadmap," we believe there are a few dos and don'ts for crafting your roadmap document.

Do:

- Make it clear what specific roadmap initiatives fall into which category (innovation, iteration, or operation). If possible, communicate the allocation target for each category as well to remind the audience the level of investment that was agreed upon.
- Paint a picture far enough in the future that it helps other teams to plan accordingly. For example, marketing may need to start working on communication plans for a large product release well in advance.
- Clarify the rationale behind the work you're planning on doing. The problems you are solving, the value you

are attempting to create, and the key outcomes you are trying to deliver are often more important than the features you currently intend to build.

- Leave room for plans to shift. Development timelines are notoriously difficult to predict in advance. As you experiment and validate assumptions through customer discovery, you will want to be able to react to what you learn, and the roadmap should allow for that.

Don't:

- Try to predict development plans so far ahead that you'll almost certainly change them before you get there. Offering this false precision is a common way to erode trust between product and the rest of the company.
- Worry about providing the same level of fidelity for every team. It's okay for the roadmap to have a "ragged edge" in which some items are better understood than others, or some teams' plans extend farther into the future than others.
- Make commitments that are unnecessary or that are unlikely to actually be met. Generally speaking, it's better to avoid feature-date pairs unless there's a specific business reason the date is as important as what actually ships.
- Get in the habit of playing roadmap Tetris to force as much in as possible. It's far better to under-commit and over-deliver than vice versa, and you'll need some buffer to accommodate the ripple effects when development doesn't go according to plan.

Communicating the Roadmap Internally

When you communicate the roadmap, we encourage you to share it with your executives first, because if you get buy-in from leaders in the organization, they can help build agreement and excitement about its contents with the rest of the employees.

Of course, you need to regularly present the roadmap to the whole company, too. However, you should consider presenting it to each major group within the company *separately* with different meetings for each of the following groups:

- Engineering, QA, and architecture
- Sales and marketing
- Account management, customer success, and customer support
- Everyone else not in those groups (HR, finance, etc.)

This allows you to speak to the specific needs and concerns that various teams might have, which helps everyone get what they need out of the presentation. For example, technical debt resolution or re-architecture that engineering needs to understand and plan for will go over the heads of virtually everyone else, and other teams won't care about anything that doesn't directly provide customer-facing value. It's also a good idea to create a forum where you can answer questions and get feedback from new hires specifically because they might have unique experiences or perspectives that can be incorporated into the next roadmap update.

We've all been in meetings where the speaker asks for questions and no hands go up. Some people don't feel comfortable asking questions or offering feedback in front of others. To overcome this inherent shyness, we've conducted surveys after our roadmap presentations because people often feel more confident sharing what they *really* think when it's private or anonymous.

Communicating the Roadmap Externally

Should you communicate your product roadmap with customers or partners? This is an area of debate in the software world. It certainly makes sense to communicate the roadmap internally to your teams, showing them what product management is doing so they can align their efforts toward the same goal, but is there value in publishing it externally?

Many people in our industry say, "No, never." However, we believe there are some situations where you might want to. For example, if you're selling an enterprise SaaS product where customers plan to use your product for many years, those customers will want to know where your product is headed. In an enterprise deal, the customer is buying the product as it works today and the vision of where you're headed. If you fail to provide that vision or roadmap, they'll fill the gap with random, ad hoc feature requests.

Many companies recognize this need, but then make a grave error in how they accommodate it. While there may be good reasons for articulating an external-facing roadmap to customers, it should never be as detailed as the internal roadmap. Your internal roadmap might include specific dates, detailed feature descriptions which are still subject to change based on continued customer research, bug fixes, and technical debt you're going to resolve, but all of these things can cause problems if you communicate them to customers.

As a general rule, if communicating a specific detail about internal plans won't drive more revenue for the product, then you shouldn't communicate it. The risk is far too high that you end up over-promising now and under-delivering later. There may be cases where a customer wants some indication that your product is going to grow along with them, in which case, your external-facing roadmap becomes essentially a marketing document to provide that reassurance. Even so, it's a good idea to remove much of the detail and depth and focus on broader themes of product development instead. If you insist on sharing dates, buffer them to give yourself some breathing room. Instead of saying, "We plan to deliver this new configuration option in July," you can simply promise to invest in configurability over the next year.

Whatever you do, don't let your salespeople take the internal roadmap and share it in an effort to close more deals. This is very dangerous. Once customers have seen your internal road-map, they're going to hold you to it, which eliminates any of the flexibility that you need as a product manager and strips away one of the most important benefits of Agile development. You might want to adjust your roadmap along the way, and the last thing you need is for customers to hold your feet to the fire when it comes to your own R&D efforts. Therefore, if you decide to communicate a roadmap to customers, minimize the amount of information you share and give yourself as much flexibility as possible.

Software Development Methodologies

There are numerous processes you can use to design, develop, and test your product. Each one approaches product management in a different way, and the one you should use depends largely on your situation. For the innovation category, you might consider doubling or tripling your normal sprint cycle and letting a cross-functional team of product, design, and engineering focus on a single new feature for that entire time, giving them the space to think outside the box, but setting a time limit so they know they need to put *something* in front of customers or users to ensure they're on the right track. For the iteration category, Scrum might make the most sense because it's well-suited for a Lean "build-measure-learn loop" and A/B testing. For the operation category, you might use Kanban to ensure production issues are handled in real-time, first in-first out.

Rajesh's Story
INNOVATION SPRINTS

At HelloWallet and Morningstar, we used to reserve some product development capacity each quarter for exploring new ideas and technologies in the form of Innovation Sprints. There were only a few rules for product, design, engineering, and QA during our one-week Innovation Sprints:

- You had to work on at least one innovation project and demo it at the end of the sprint.

- Teams were self-forming. On the first day, there was a pitch-a-thon to recruit colleagues to help you with your project idea(s).
- If you planned to push a change to production, you needed a full squad (product, design, engineering, and QA), and the change had to be ready to deploy by the end of the sprint.

As a part of its Agile transformation, Morningstar renovated one of the floors in their Chicago headquarters to house a small amphitheater explicitly for sprint demos. I remember sitting in that amphitheater, watching an amazing demo from a front-end engineer and a designer. They had made a mobile responsive version of our new robo-advisor web app in a week! It wasn't production-ready, but they demoed the entire workflow in a couple of minutes. As we were walking out, I thought about how they were able to make such a big change in such a short time and concluded that it was a combination of:

- Motivation (they chose to work on it)
- Freedom (no one told them *how* to collaborate, and there weren't a million Jira tickets to keep track of)
- Focus (they didn't do anything else for that week but sit next to each other and jam on this idea)

While you might not always be able to provide all three, take a minute to talk to your team about whether any game-changing process improvements might make a huge difference in how your team ships customer and business value. You may also consider asking the team to draft their ideal process and identify action items to close the biggest gaps from how they work today.

Assessing Product Development Efficiency

As we've said, the efficiency with which you can deliver something doesn't matter if what you're delivering is of little or no value. But when you are working on the right things, then the efficiency with which you deliver matters plenty.

Though output is less important than outcomes, you still need to measure your speed of progress somehow. Many people like to use Scrum story points for measuring progress, which assigns point values to various pieces of work based on complexity, but we think it's more important and more useful to track the percentage of the roadmap that you have completed.

Demo in Reverse

The Scrum methodology is based on work being done in sprints. Let's suppose you're conducting a two-week sprint. At the end of those two weeks, all of the engineers get together and demo to each other and the product manager what they've built, and everyone applauds.

Personally, we feel like it's a bit one-sided to make engineers demo to product managers. Why don't the product managers have to demo anything to the engineers? Instead, product managers just submit requests and then there is a sort of handshake agreement that the engineers will build products and features that are functional, scalable, and meet expectations, as long as the product managers don't change priorities mid-sprint.

Shouldn't product managers also be held accountable for not wasting the engineers' time on meaningless requests that don't actually help customers or move the business forward? We believe that after engineers have released features (or other enhancements) to production that had been intended to move a particular metric or deliver some value, the product manager should come back with evidence that the outcome was actually delivered. If the work was an experiment, then they should find out what was learned from it. Engineers deserve to know that the work they're doing isn't a waste of time. Whatever the intended outcome of the request—raising a business metric, adding customer value, learning something—product managers should show them the impact of the work they did. Think of it as a demo in reverse.

We don't think this is necessary for every sprint. That's far too frequent and usually doesn't give the product improvement that was delivered enough time in-market to show results. However, once a quarter is probably about right. Sadly, this is almost never done, but we feel like it should be an industry-wide practice for product managers and something engineering teams deserve.

CREATING AND MANAGING THE
PRODUCT METRICS DASHBOARD

As a product leader, you should be able to look beyond specific product updates and see how the product is performing as a whole. This means creating a metrics dashboard showing your key outcome metrics, both for the company and for the customer, and reviewing it on a regular basis.

Beware of making your dashboard too complicated. We see many product dashboards that are so overloaded with metrics that they strain the eye. We recommend keeping it very simple, tracking just a few key metrics related to your outcome pyramid and updating it daily.

Consider including temporary performance metrics that are relevant to what you're currently working on. For example, maybe you just had a big product launch that was supposed to drive a specific metric. Add it to the dashboard for a while after launch so you can track whether or not the product launch had its intended impact and then remove it again after it's been determined and the results have become absorbed into the broader dashboard measurements.

Finally, we recommend exposing your dashboard internally and reviewing the metrics regularly, so there is true transparency in your organization about the progress you're making. Since your teams know these things are being tracked, they will keep these metrics in mind as they make decisions in their daily work. In that way, you draw a direct connection between the individual efforts of individuals in the product, design, and engineering teams and the overall measure of success or failure that is being presented regularly.

ACTION CHECKLIST AND RESOURCES

Visit *buildwhatmattersbook.com* for an action checklist and resources to help you set up the processes, workshops, and metrics dashboard discussed in this chapter.

CHAPTER EIGHT

THE RIGHT TEAM

"If you want to go fast, go alone.
If you want to go far, go together."

—African Proverb

Having the right processes in place won't do much good if you don't have the right people in place to implement them, so building your product teams requires careful consideration.

The organizational structure of a product team tends to evolve with the growth of a company. In an early-stage startup, the founder is responsible for everything product-related, such as setting the vision, prioritizing, talking to users, pitching customers on value, and sometimes even specifying product details for the engineering team. Eventually, however, as the company matures, the founder will necessarily delegate some of these responsibilities to other roles.

As your company and product mature, responsibilities will evolve, and your organizational structure is going to change.

You can think about all of the specific responsibilities in an organization as balls being juggled. In the beginning, the founder has a lot of balls in the air at once. Once you hire your first product manager, many of those are going to be juggled by that person, so make sure you hire someone who's capable. Then, as your organization grows further, different people will take on the responsibility for keeping the other balls in the air, and as some responsibilities expand, the number of balls will multiply.

As the graphic on the following page makes clear, there are different phases of a product team's evolution, beginning with the first hire.

MAKING YOUR FIRST PRODUCT HIRE

For that first hire, some founders make the mistake of bringing in a vice president of product management or chief product officer (CPO). We believe this is problematic because it creates tension between the product executive and the founder at a time when the company is still the founder's baby. This is almost always too early for the founder to hand the keys over to someone else.

Instead, your first hire should usually be a senior product manager (SPM), someone who can follow your vision and strategy without a lot of handholding. Working together, a senior product manager can help you develop and execute a balanced roadmap. How can you tell when it's time to hire your first product manager? Generally, there are four clues to look for.

The Evolution of a Product Team

BALLS TO JUGGLE

TEAM 1

FOUNDER / CEO

❶ Vision / Strategy
❷ Roadmap Execution
❸ Customer Journey
❹ People

TEAM 2

FOUNDER / CEO

❶ Vision / Strategy
❹ People

SR PM

❷ Roadmap Execution
❸ Customer Journey

TEAM 3

FOUNDER / CEO

❶ Vision / Strategy
❹ People

SR PM

❷ Roadmap Execution

DESIGNER

❸ Customer Journey

TEAM 4

FOUNDER / CEO

❶ Company Vision / Strategy
❹ People (Execs / Board)

VP PRODUCT

❺ Product Vision / Strategy
❻ Product People

SR PM   SR PM

DESIGNER

❷ Roadmap Execution

❸ Customer Journey

First, founders usually try to stay actively involved in product development, but at some point, fundraising, hiring, and operations start to dominate their schedules. If you no longer have time to spend on product management activities, that's a big clue it's time to hire a product manager.

Second, if you've started worrying that the engineering team is working on the wrong things, it might be time for your first product hire. Maybe you find you disagree with certain prioritization choices that have been delegated to the engineering team, or you raise an eyebrow when looking over the latest release notes. If you're not certain that your team is delivering maximum value, you probably need to hire a product manager.

Third, if you've reached a point where you have five or more engineers, you need a product manager. Engineers are often your most expensive team members, so you want to make sure they are focused on the right priorities. Why do we use five as the threshold? The first reason is that it's definitely enough engineering capacity to keep a product manager busy full time. The second reason comes down to simple math. Suppose you pay your engineers $120,000 a year. That means you're spending $600,000 per year on engineering. If 25 percent of what they're working on isn't high-priority, that's $150,000, which should be more than enough to hire a solid senior product manager to reduce that percentage.

Fourth, if you're launching a second product, you will need to hire in product, if you haven't already. The challenge of context switching, wrangling priorities for innovation, iteration, and operation across products that are at different lifecycle stages, can overwhelm a team that is operating without a dedicated product manager. You will need someone to conduct customer discovery interviews, handle customer feature requests, identify usability issues, review quantitative usage data, evaluate the competition, and then determine the right priorities across all of these disparate inputs, and none of this should come from an engineer or executive who needs to concentrate their efforts elsewhere.

Hiring your first product manager is a major turning point. Make it very clear what the scope and boundaries of their role are. Think very carefully about this first hire, because the ramifications will be enormous for your company. You don't want to get two years down the road and realize that a bad hire for your first product manager has taken the product in the wrong direction or created technical debt that could plague you for years to come.

WHAT TO LOOK FOR WHEN MAKING YOUR FIRST PRODUCT HIRE

In our work as advisors for many startups, we've worked with hundreds of product managers. Some have been highly experienced, some fresh out of school, and others pulled in from other positions at the company or nonproduct positions elsewhere. And in doing so, we've seen one consistent characteristic that separated the great product managers from the ones who've perpetually struggled. It's not experience, domain knowledge, technical expertise, or anything else so easily identified on a resume. In our opinion, a strong *product mindset* is the single most important characteristic of a product management hire. When evaluating their mindset, look for these key attributes:

- Customer empathy
- Curiosity
- Humility
- Adaptability
- Intelligence
- Data-driven decision-making
- Continuous improvement
- Scrappiness

One of the best product managers we've ever worked with was on Ben's team at Opower. His intense curiosity was his superpower. When he first became a product manager, he had no idea how the technology worked, so he sat down with the engineers and talked with them at length, then followed up by reading books and watching videos about anything he didn't fully understand. In fact, he got to a point where he had a better technical understanding of the product than some of the engineers. He was able to figure out exactly what data he needed to make smart decisions, and when he couldn't access it through existing reports, he learned SQL to pull the data himself. He never gave excuses for not delivering results, and instead offered creative ideas for how to improve the next time around.

Many of the best product managers have little formal experience in product management, no certifications or advanced degrees, no prior exposure to the domain, and sometimes start with insufficient understanding of the technology and business acumen. The ones who succeed are the ones self-directed and motivated to learn everything they need, ask the right questions, take accountability for outcomes, and refuse to quit.

You might consider moving someone from another function within your organization into an associate product management (APM) role. The tough part is determining whether or not an internal hire in another function has potential. Through the work they've been doing in their current role, have they exhibited a product mindset? Do you have reason to believe they will be a good product manager based on things they've said or an interest they've shown?

THE VALUE OF HOMEWORK ASSIGNMENTS

We strongly recommend that you give homework assignments to all prospective product management hires. We realize this is a controversial topic. Indeed, some leaders are dead set against the idea, but we believe it is one of the most tried-and-true ways of separating great candidates from good ones. One of the most important considerations for any product management hire is product mindset, but how can you evaluate a person's mindset from a resume and a conversation? This is something best revealed through an exercise.

It's easy for a prospective hire to hand you a resume that rattles off all of their accomplishments and the business impact they've had, but the truth is, product managers work in cross-functional teams. When you read about their past accomplishments, you don't know if they drove them or if they were simply along for the ride. A homework assignment gives you a way to see the real value of a prospective hire because it's something that they do by themselves. It's amazing how often a candidate who looks great on paper will utterly fail a homework assignment.

One of the top reasons product leaders hesitate to give homework is because they worry that it will scare off a good candidate. In all honesty, this is a possibility, but we've only seen it happen a handful of times out of hundreds and hundreds of interviews. In a few instances, when a good prospective hire resisted doing a homework assignment, we waived the requirement and conducted the interview anyway, but their reluctance to do the homework translated into a broader reluctance to roll up their sleeves and get their hands dirty at the whiteboard.

As for the assignment itself, it should present a real business challenge that your company is currently facing or has faced. Don't give the candidate some weird math homework that has nothing to do with your company or feels more like an aptitude test versus a real case study. You want to see how they would perform in the role, but you also want to give them a clear indication of the type of work they will be doing. Ideally, they will walk away from the assignment saying either, "This is exactly the kind of work I want to be doing," or "This is not for me." That's a realization that is better had before they start working for you, or even before they waste a day of their time (and yours) in in-person interviews.

Don't ask a candidate to spend more than two or three hours on a homework assignment. You're not looking for a polished response, anyway. Even if they just provide a half-baked idea for solving a problem, that's perfectly fine, because you can use it as the basis for discussions during the interview process. Instead of simply peppering them with a bunch of textbook interview questions about their prior experience, you can now address a relevant product decision that they've made on a problem you're both familiar with.

"Why did you make this decision? What kind of data would you collect to validate this assumption? If you had to drop something from the MVP to make an accelerated deadline, what would it be? Why?" By answering these kinds of questions, they will show you how they think rather than merely telling you what they expect you to want to hear.

What you're offering candidates is the opportunity to show-case their product mindset, which includes hard-to-find traits that the greatest product managers possess. A well-designed assignment will help you discover them during the in-person interview process.

MAKING YOUR SECOND PRODUCT HIRE

Your second product hire will generally occur when you're launching a new product. This could be a junior or associate product manager (APM) who can take over the simpler or more steady-state portions of the product while the senior PM goes to work on the more complex challenge.

This is a good opportunity to add strength where it is conspic-uously missing in the first product manager, and begin balancing the team early on. Ideally, each product manager will be able to learn from the other due to differences in experience, skillset, communication styles, and so on. Consider looking for someone with a differing seniority level than the first product manager. If your first product manager was relatively senior, or perhaps a company co-founder, consider hiring someone more junior.

Hiring a Product Executive

Adding a second product manager is the right time to also *consider* hiring a product executive, such as a VP or director of product, to begin assuming responsibility for the broader roadmap or important strategic decisions that will fulfill the founder's vision. If you choose to hire a VP of product while hiring your second product manager, it's probably best to hire the VP first so they can hire the kind of product manager they want as they begin to build out their team.

A VP of product makes sense when the CEO or founder is no longer able to focus on the product strategy because they're too busy running the company. We don't recommend considering it until you have an MVP, at least a few satisfied paying customers, *and* at least two product managers. At some point, the founder will have so many priorities that the advantages of delegating strategy and eventually vision to someone else outweigh the disadvantages.

Of course, you also need the funding to support such a hire. A VP of product is an expensive hire, and it's not a hands-on position. Unless you're asking them to play a hybrid role, this individual will be leading and managing, not working directly with the engineering team to ship product. Can your budget support such a hire, and is that the best use of scarce capital? It might be, or perhaps the prudent choice is to wait for the next round of funding.

For the VP of product to succeed, the CEO or founder must be ready to delegate product strategy decisions. For a smooth handoff, we recommend you wait until market feedback confirms you are headed in the right direction with your vision and strategy, as it's difficult to hand off such important responsibilities while they are still forming or highly unstable.

Case Study

WESPIRE: PRODUCT RESPONSIBILITIES OF THE CEO

In 2012, WeSpire was in the midst of a successful pivot from a B2C model to an enterprise model, where their sustainability engagement software was bought by companies to use with their employees. The founder and CEO, Susan Hunt Stevens, shared with us her story about hiring a product leader too soon. In her own words:

"We were a very small, but highly nimble team early on consisting, on the product side, of me, our CTO and our lead product designer backed by a great team of engineers. We joked that we made the perfect startup leadership team—an artist, a hustler, and a hacker. We worked incredibly closely together, made decisions on the fly, and in general, we were experiencing some incredible success.

"However, as Founder and CEO, I was also chief sales officer, chief fundraiser, CFO, and wore numerous other hats. The more I got pulled away from the office onto the road for various reasons, and the more customers we added, the more our CTO was feeling the pain of my absence. He felt we needed someone to be helping him on day-to-day decisions. What he described sounded to me like a product leader.

"So I went and hired a great head of product and delegated all product responsibilities to her immediately. I thought this was what was needed to scale, but within a couple months, everyone was miserable and we ultimately had to part ways. In hindsight, it wasn't her fault. It was just way too early for us to bring in a head of product.

"Given I was the person out speaking to customers and prospects the most and I had the vision for what this business and product was going to be and do, the company needed *me* to continue to play the head of product role. What we had really needed at that stage was more of an individual contributor product manager who could execute. It was a hard lesson to learn, but I'm glad we did. We've kept product and tech leadership together at this stage, without a separate head of product, and will likely do so until we double in size again."

ESTABLISHING DESIGN

As your product team grows, you will quickly find that design needs to be its own function separate from product management. We recommend this split in responsibilities as soon as the company can afford the additional headcount. For example, a common early stage product organization might have two product managers and one product designer, who is responsible for user experience (UX) design and user interface (UI) design. What's the difference between UX design and UI (or visual) design? Both are components of the "front end" that your users will interact with, but they are different disciplines requiring different skillsets.

UX design more broadly addresses topics like product usability: how users will perform essential tasks, find information where they expect it, get up and running quickly without becoming overwhelmed, and so on. UX design usually involves heavy user research to understand users' mental models and expectations and then work with product management to design the experiences within the product so they are highly usable. UX design tends to work on mock-ups and prototypes using tools like Sketch and InVision.

UI design, or visual design, more broadly addresses topics like the visual look and feel of the product, how the product experience mirrors the brand elements, the consistency of frequently used styles, the use of animations for usability and delight, and so on. UI design establishes and maintains a visual style guide for product development, but also contributes directly to usability by directing users' attention to the right points at the right time and defining repeatable design patterns that flatten the learning curve for new features. UI design is the function that builds visual assets, like design systems that include buttons, graphics, icons, and animation patterns.

Just as product design usually splinters off of product management early on, as the team matures, UX design and UI design will decouple, too. The required backgrounds and skillsets are actually quite different, so finding a designer in the early days capable of doing both well can be a real challenge. If you can find a designer who can also conduct customer research, they could easily become one of your most important individual contributors, even if they are a consultant.

Once the design function grows to two or three people, we find it's better to avoid having designers report into individual product managers. Both functions should report to the head of product, but there are advantages of having design operate independently from product management. A peer relationship between the two functions better reflects the way they should collaborate, and it gives UX/UI design a stronger voice in the roadmapping process.

SCALING A PRODUCT ORGANIZATION

As teams expand, you'll want to achieve and maintain the right balance between product management, design, engineering, and quality assurance personnel. While this varies from situation to situation based on the nature of the product and its lifecycle, we generally recommend the following ratios for each team:

- 5 to 7 Developers (your base value)
- 1 Product Manager
- 0.5 UX Designer (variable depending on the nature of the product)
- 0.3 UI Designer (variable depending on the nature of the product)
- 1 or 2 Quality Assurance Engineers

In other words, for every five to seven developers, add one dedicated product manager, half a UX designer, one-third of a visual/UI designer and one or two QA engineers. We like to use software engineers as the base value because everyone knows how many engineers they have and it's engineers who actually produce working code.

Many earlier stage companies experience rapid growth, increasing their staff by fifty percent or more each year. Some can grow several hundred percent year over year! In cases of hypergrowth, where the team size is constantly increasing, we strongly advise staffing your product management team today to match the number of engineers you *expect to have* in three to six months because in a product-driven company, product managers tend to work well ahead of engineers. If you're currently balanced but expect to have twelve more engineers in six months, for example, then you should hire two more product managers now, so those product managers have time to figure out customer needs and product priorities, and the next wave of engineers can hit the ground running when they start.

As the number of product managers grows to match the number of scrum teams, it's easy to create confusion about who has jurisdiction over decisions and major portions of the product. The product leader needs to take the time to over-communicate the lines of responsibility so that product managers don't clobber each other and so that parts of the product that require an owner actually have one. For example, if a high-severity bug gets filed, whose duty is it to prioritize it in their backlog? Who is responsible for resolving technical debt buried deep in the code that's causing database performance issues? These questions require answers from product management and engineering leaders.

As product teams continue to grow, you may find that an intermediate management level of product management is needed. For most product management teams, a manager can only effectively support about five to six direct reports. So, a team of twenty-five product managers may require five directors of product management as mid-level managers. The director-level function in product management is complex because directors are neither hands-on managing a scrum team, nor are they responsible for the overarching product vision and strategy. Their job usually entails the following responsibilities:

- Hiring, firing, retaining, and coaching team members
- Interpreting portions of the strategy and taking accountability for delivering against strategic milestones that require collaboration across multiple scrum teams
- Understanding the middle parts of the outcome pyramids and taking accountability for demonstrating ROI by growing customer outcomes and business success metrics

PRODUCT OWNER VERSUS PRODUCT MANAGER

A common pattern we see as the product team scales, especially in larger organizations or companies selling into the enterprise space, is to split the product function into two distinct roles: a product manager and a product owner. The delineation is fairly standard:

- **The product manager** is responsible for understanding the market opportunity, competitive landscape, customer needs, and success metrics, and then makes the strategic and prioritization decisions, handing them off to the product owner.

- **The product owner** fulfills obligations to the engineering team by specifying requirements and acceptance criteria, managing the backlog, attending daily stand-up meetings with their respective scrum teams, and dealing with issues in development as they arise.

In this model, there is generally a hierarchy in which the product manager is the more senior role and sometimes the product owners report directly to the product managers. The primary benefit of this approach is that one party can spend time with customers learning and making strategic decisions while the other can be available to the engineering team 24/7 and focus on execution and delivery.

However, in our experience, the cons outweigh the pros. Downsides include:

- Playing a game of continuous telephone since neither party can make informed decisions on their own, but both need to be involved
- No one person having full accountability for delivering outcomes
- Potentially disempowering the engineering team by making them one step farther removed from customers
- Having "too many cooks in the kitchen," resulting in bloated processes and budgets

Almost none of the more modern Silicon Valley startups follow this model for all these reasons, and while we often advise companies who have already committed to this organizational structure and can attest to its merits, we have never *recommended* it to a company contemplating the decision.

THE ROLE OF PRODUCT OPERATIONS

There's a relatively new product role that's getting a lot of attention these days called *product operations*. The purpose of product operations is to make the teams as effective as possible by centralizing the functions that should be defined and executed consistently and providing necessary support for the functions that are better decentralized.

Examples of the responsibilities that can be delegated to product ops include:

- Composing internal-facing product documentation, release notes, and training materials
- Organizing regular meetings to collect stakeholder input for product roadmap updates
- Procuring software tools and systems used by product managers and UX design
- Collecting and evaluating product management efficiency metrics
- Maintaining and publicizing the product metrics dashboard
- Training new product managers
- Providing knowledge-sharing opportunities across the product management team

- Creating, implementing, and enforcing policies (for example, a checklist of stakeholders to be notified prior to a major release going to production)
- Setting processes for pulling engineers and designers into product decisions early

The product ops role makes a lot of sense for larger or more mature organizations, where there are numerous product managers and processes that could be made more efficient.

Ben's Story
THE IMPACT OF PRODUCT OPS

When I arrived at Opower, the need for a product ops position was immediately apparent. Salespeople didn't understand important product features, there was very little internal product documentation, there was no onboarding and training plan for the five product managers I needed to hire; the list went on and on. However, back in 2010, this was a role no one had heard of. I had never seen it described, so I struggled with basic decisions like what to name the position and what to put in the job description. In presenting it to the executive team to secure funding, I met plenty of resistance. "Wait, you're going to hire someone who will work *with* product managers but won't write code and won't be a product manager themselves? What are they going to do?" It was a tough sell.

Thankfully, I was given the benefit of the doubt, and the first person I interviewed for the role was a superstar. Although there was plenty of confusion (even from me) about the value this role would deliver to the organization before he was hired, it became obvious to everyone within just two weeks. Suddenly, we had an audit of our Agile practices and recommendations for improvement. We had a well-organized space set up in Confluence (Atlassian's wiki that complements JIRA). We had consolidated release notes spanning all product managers that explained, in terms stakeholders could understand, not only what was being released, but how to adjust sales demos and talk about it with current clients.

That was just the beginning. From there, we were able to do far more advanced work that was instrumental in allowing the company to scale at a hypergrowth pace. Product ops built tracking into our wiki so we could see which content was actually being used or not. We created short videos explaining advanced product features in simple terms that account managers could use on their own or share with clients. We analyzed the predictability of delivering roadmap items and associated business outcomes according to plan and measured improvement against those success rates as we continued to evolve our processes.

Centralization of specific operational functions within product management allowed everyone to be much more productive both inside and outside of the product team. Just as importantly, as the product leader, delegating these operational tasks and processes freed me up to focus on more forward-looking product strategy.

CONWAY'S LAW

According to Conway's Law, which was developed by software programmer Melvin Conway, "Any organization that designs a system will produce a design whose structure is a copy of the organization's communication structure."[4] In other words, what teams deliver will be a reflection of their organizational structure. In our experience as advisors, Conway's Law has usually proven true with almost every team we've worked with.

When setting the structure of your organization, you need to understand, analyze, and carefully consider the impact it will have on the product you deliver to customers. If you're destined to ship a product that reflects your team structure, then the seams in your organizational structure will be replicated in the user experience. For example, if one team develops your desktop app and a different team develops the mobile version of that app, and the teams don't collaborate well, then you're likely to wind up with two very different user experiences. Customers who have learned the desktop version of the app will find the transition to the mobile app jarring and wonder why the experience feels so disjointed. If, instead, you organize your team so that one product manager is responsible for customer acquisition, and another is responsible for user engagement of paid accounts, then there's a good chance that customers will experience inconsistency when they migrate from a trial account to paid.

---

4 "Conway's Law," Mel Conway, accessed March 24, 2020, http://www.melconway.com/Home/Conways_Law.html.

There is no silver bullet solution. The trick is to minimize the negative consequences by placing the seams in the organization where they will have the least impact on your ability to deliver customer outcomes and business results. It's also possible through good management oversight from the product and engineering leaders to spot situations in which Conway's Law is having an adverse effect on technology, user experience design, etc. and to smooth out the bumps, but be aware that they probably won't ever go away completely.

ORGANIZING A TEAM OF PRODUCT MANAGERS

As your team grows, you have to create seams somewhere, so where do you want them? We propose six general ways of structuring your teams:

- By product
- By feature
- By technical layer
- By customer segment or persona
- By customer journey stage
- By performance metric

In order to illustrate these different organizational approaches, we'll explain and contrast them through the example of Uber since it's familiar to most readers (but we recognize Uber is large and complex, and we are not actually suggesting a structure that would be overly simplistic for them at this stage).

Organizing by Product

At larger companies with multiple products on the market, it's easy to break the work down by product. However, confusion about what constitutes a "product" can trip teams up. We define a product as something people use to help them achieve an outcome that they find important.

For example, Uber offers a number of distinct products: the original ride-sharing service, Uber Eats, and JUMP scooters. For Uber, organizing by product would mean having a product manager (or, more likely, teams of product managers) for each of these products.

Organizing by Feature

An organizational structure can also be built around product features. You are probably aware that the Uber app has a number of different features: booking a ride, real-time driver tracking, payment options, driver reviews, trip history, and so on. Imagine assigning a product manager to each of these features.

Although this is a common way of organizing teams, it creates dependencies as some feature changes might require development work from multiple feature teams, which slows down the delivery of value to the customer.

Organizing by Technical Layer

This organizational structure typically has distinct teams built around three common layers of software products: data, APIs, and user interface. Sometimes, it revolves around individual operating systems—iPhone, Android, Web—with specific teams focusing on each form factor and a back-end team supporting all three. The engineering team holds a lot of sway in these kinds of organizations.

The problem with this structure is that it becomes almost impossible to ship anything. One of our clients told the story of an iOS feature that was recently demoed. A team member was impressed and asked, "This looks great, when will users see it?" The product team replied, "Oh, this was just the front-end work. Our back-end team didn't have time to finish their work yet, so we won't be able to ship for at least another two or three months."

This is a classic example of *dependency hell.* It looks like the product team has created something, but there's another team lagging behind due to a different set of competing priorities. Consequently, despite appearances, no actual value has been delivered to customers. In fact, one of the reasons why enterprise companies move so slowly is that they have convoluted organizational structures with multiple teams, each one moving at their own pace. This is a major reason why startups have been able to catch up to large, established companies, despite their advantages. Teams in bloated organizations may be able to move fast individually, but not together.

Organizing by Customer Segment or Persona

Rather than organizing around products, you can organize your teams according to your customer segments or personas. Imagine if Uber had a product manager for specific customer segments such as: full-time professional drivers, occasional drivers, business travelers, partiers, and families with children. A different product manager would be assigned to achieving success for each specific user type.

For other companies, customers might instead be segmented as buyer versus user, enterprise versus SMB, or client versus supplier. Whatever the case, this is a good way to focus teams on the needs of users, but it requires heavy coordination across teams to avoid duplicating efforts, deviating from established design principles, or taking the product in different directions at the same time.

Organizing by Customer Journey Stage

In this organizational structure, you have a different product manager for each major part of the experience, such as discovery, trial (including conversion to paid), engagement, retention, and so on. This structure focuses attention on key elements of the customer journey, naturally aligning product managers to the fulfillment of the vision. Often, there are also important business metrics that closely mirror the success or failure of customers continuing their journey at those junctures, allowing for delegation of accountability. However, this structure requires a lot of design coordination to ensure a cohesive customer experience. For example, you wouldn't want first-time users of Uber to encounter different verbiage within the app from premium users, and you wouldn't want buttons or dropdown menus to work differently as users become progressively more engaged.

Organizing by Performance Metric

It's also possible to organize product teams based on specific product metrics. For example, Uber might consider organizing the product management group by key performance indicators, such as a product manager focused on revenue from new customer acquisition, another product manager focused on customer average revenue per account (ARPA), and a third product manager focused on net promoter score (NPS). The main benefit of this approach is pushing accountability to individual product managers, but it can result in multiple teams wanting (or needing) to work on the same product components at the same time and no one feeling ownership for the design quality of specific features that those teams collaborate on.

Summary of Organizational Options

Key Considerations for Product Development Org Structure

Org Structure	Pros	Cons	Best Suited For
Product	• Very clear which team should handle specific feedback/bugs • Easy to bring the right product person to external product meetings, such as a sales call	• Constrains vision/strategy/roadmap to product level (not very customer-centric) • Requires a lot of cross-team coordination when products are tightly integrated with each other	Companies with multiple products with limited dependencies
Features	• Very clear which team should handle specific feedback/bugs • Fewer dependencies than other options	• Causes confusion when features require infrastructure/architectural updates • Constrains vision/strategy/roadmap to feature level (not very customer-centric)	Companies with mature products with several meaty features

Org Structure	Pros	Cons	Best Suited For
Technical Layers	• Aligns with engineering team specialties, such as front-end or iOS • Very clear which team should handle specific feedback/bugs	• Creates confusing UX due to unrationalized feature discrepancies across technical layers (ex. feature on web not available on mobile) • Requires a lot of cross-team roadmap coordination to manage dependencies	Companies with a highly technical or complex algorithmic product
Customer Segments/ Personas	• Very customer-centric, encourages teams to think about customer needs/outcomes • Simplifies user research, each team can target interviews by the type of person they want to talk to and can become experts in that persona over time	• Can pull the product in multiple directions at once • Requires a lot of cross-team coordination when multiple products are sold to a customer segment	Companies who serve very different customer types with their product suite
Customer Journey Stage	• Supports growth teams well, growth teams focus on driving people to product, other teams focus on trial and engagement • Clear metrics you can assign to each product manager, such as conversion from free trial to paid or retention	• Requires tight governance to ensure a consistent and great UX across stages • Complicated for a viral growth strategy where usage serves as a trigger, discovery and evaluation for prospects	Companies with a well-defined linear customer journey and a heavy emphasis on growth

Org Structure	Pros	Cons	Best Suited For
Metrics	• Easy to assign goals to teams and then measure product success • Easy to delegate decision making and accountability amongst product managers	• Requires stable set of KPIs that won't change often • Requires cross-team roadmap coordination as individual teams may need to touch a lot of product areas to hit goals	Companies with well-established product KPIs that capture customer and business outcomes

There are pros and cons to each of the organizational structures. Here are some considerations as you decide which one is right for your company:

- Maximizing autonomy (minimizing dependencies) between teams
- Minimizing the impact of Conway's Law on your customer experience
- Creating clear jurisdictions and responsibilities for individual product managers
- Optimizing for the product life cycle stage (you may choose different org structures based on the maturity of the product)

You may also consider a hybrid approach, such as organizing by persona and metrics or having "vertical teams" for each product or feature and a "horizontal team" for the underlying platform that supports them all. Organizing a growing product team is a tricky decision for many companies, and we often get pulled in as advisors to help them make the right decision.

ESTABLISHING A HEALTHY CULTURE

There are a lot of ways to think about company culture. We like to define it as "the everyday behavior of employees." When you instill a culture of excellence within your product team, you earn the trust of your team members because your decision-making feels justified. A healthy culture provides the soil in which Vision-Led Product Management can take root and grow. To create that culture, there are a few things you need to do:

1. Dedicate time to customer discovery
2. Focus on collaboration
3. Delegate decision-making
4. Emphasize diversity

Let's look at each one of these in detail.

Dedicating Time to Customer Discovery

What is the difference between the culture of a product team at a startup and the culture of a product team in an enterprise? While most people would call out the difference in pace and nimbleness, in our experience, the most important distinguishing characteristic of the enterprise is the degree of separation that emerges between product managers and customers. Thankfully, it's something the product leader can influence directly.

If you're running a startup with just five employees, it is likely that every one of those five people has regular contact with your customers and prospects. This is incredibly beneficial in helping you build a better product because every employee understands the needs of those customers.

As the organization grows, you add a sales team, then a customer success team. Client-facing employees take over as the voice of the customer, and they usually don't want product managers interfering with their charter by asking questions of customers directly. Before you know it, a game of telephone begins to form between the product team and the customers.

Customer Interactions

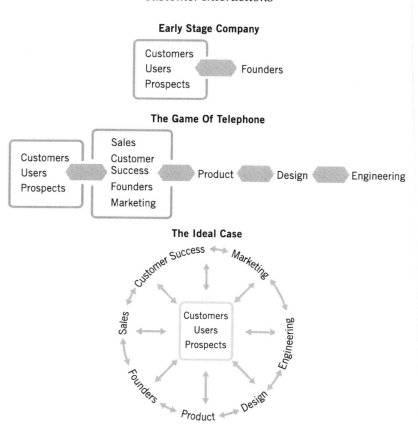

We find that enterprise product managers rarely get the chance to talk to customers, except to help close large deals, so all of their decisions are made by proxy. Sales informs them of what a customer wants, and the customer success teams say things like, "We have to deliver this new feature, or this customer is going to fire us." Product management then has no choice but to take this information at face value and respond accordingly.

The feedback can still be helpful, but without direct customer interaction outside the context of a sales process, there's no opportunity to ask follow-up questions that further reveal their motivations and the rationale behind specific feature requests. Remember the 5 *Whys*. Christian Idiodi, a partner at Silicon Valley Product Group, said something at a 2019 product conference in New York that stuck with us: "Those who have the power in a company are the ones who are perceived to be the customer experts."

If you want product management to drive the company forward, then you need to provide them with the deepest, best understanding of the customer. Here are some specific ways to ensure product managers get frequent interactions with customers:

- **Usability studies.** Ideally, product managers should conduct (or at least attend) usability studies and they should also contribute to survey content and customer interviews being done by a customer research specialist. Consider doing usability testing with prospects or customers who have never engaged to get insights from people who aren't yet familiar with the product and can provide their first impressions.

- **Sales calls.** As we discussed earlier, a product-driven company needs to have a product that's ready for the *next* customer. Understanding the needs and evaluation criteria of prospects is a key input for the product vision, strategy, and roadmap.

- **Customer check-ins.** Most account management teams do quarterly business reviews (QBRs) with customers. Having product managers join those calls lets them hear firsthand how the customer feels things are going. During these calls, the product team might also demo a new feature to get feedback or ask questions to inform the future direction of the product.

- **Site visits.** There's nothing more insightful than seeing a product in action in the real world. Understanding the environment in which the product is being used, the workflows that precede and follow product usage and the people who are "behind the clicks" arms product managers and designers with critical information they need to make the right product decisions.

- **Missed opportunity interviews.** Product managers tend to prefer speaking to customers that are relatively friendly and approachable and with whom they have a trusted long-term relationship. However, these "anchor accounts" might not be representative of the future customer you're trying to build for, so they need to speak to the silent majority as well. There are many ways to do this. For example, if someone bails on your website or app after exploring for a while, use a pop-up to offer them a $50 Amazon gift card if they will talk to a product manager for thirty minutes about what they came for and why they left. Who knows, you might even close a deal by accident!

- **Product advisory board.** Form a committee comprised of your top-tier accounts who have a good pulse on the direction of the industry. These forward-thinking customers can provide guidance on where your product should be headed and they are usually capable of separating their own idiosyncratic requests from their thoughts on future product direction, serving as a good proxy for the market as a whole.

Focusing on Collaboration

In a healthy culture, product managers collaborate well with others. Technically, being a successful product manager means clearly defining what success looks like and hitting goals related to that definition, but product is such a collaborative process that a product manager also needs to listen and to exhibit empathy. Otherwise, they might end up steamrolling people and creating a toxic environment.

Do your colleagues respect you, enjoy working with you, and consider you a great collaborator? If you're not sure, you might consider conducting a simple 360-degree feedback survey of the people who collaborate with you:

- On a scale of 1 to 5 (with 1 being *horrible* and 5 being *excellent*), how am I doing as a product manager?
- What am I doing well? Please provide specific examples.
- What could I be doing better? Please provide specific examples.

Getting feedback from people you work with every day can be uncomfortable, but it's a good way to discover how you're doing and identify opportunities for improving. You may not be the great collaborator you think you are, in which case some changes might be in order.

Still, don't forget that the product manager is the decision-maker. Ultimately, successful leadership is not about making everyone like you. If that were the measure of success, you could just offer an open bar or free ice cream every afternoon! In reality, you want your team to *trust* that your decisions are sound, that there's a rationale behind them, and that you are aligned to a vision and strategy that make sense for the customer and the company. It's less about being *nice* and more about being *effective*.

Delegating Decision-Making

A healthy culture uses KPIs and the organizational structure to push decisions down to individual contributors. By having a set of KPIs, as the company scales, the VP of product or chief product officer can hand individual metrics to product managers, empowering them to make decisions and innovate to hit their goals.

A culture of innovation gives people the space, time, tools, and resources to understand problems and opportunities thoroughly and think creatively about solutions. Do you allow people to make their own decisions by providing clarity, removing roadblocks, and giving context, or do you enforce more of a "command and control" environment?

Emphasizing Diversity

As you begin bringing in new people to fill out your product team, we strongly encourage taking active steps to invest in diversity. This includes diversity across gender, race, age, socio-economics, religion, sexual orientation, and more. Appropriate representation is both a matter of ethics *and* a matter of maximizing your business performance.

Returning to what constitutes a product-driven company, the product manager must be willing to *interpret* what they hear from customers, users, and stakeholders rather than taking everything at face value. This need to interpret what they see and hear amplifies the importance of product management having broad perspective. Everyone is subject to their cognitive biases, implicit biases, and the life experiences that have shaped them over the years. Working in isolation or with a team of lookalikes, a product manager cannot help but introduce these biases into their prioritization and design decisions. However, working together with a diverse team, *especially on the dimensions of race and gender*, can provide the necessary counterbalances and distinct points of view that are necessary for product managers shouldering the responsibility that comes with working in a product-driven company.

With that in mind, when we talk about diversity, we also include personality, perspective, thought processes, and experience. Product sits at the intersection of business, design, and technology. Creating a mix of product managers, some with experience as senior developers, others who have studied design, and others with a strong business management background, contributes to diversity and overall team effectiveness.

Unfortunately, lack of diversity in product teams is a widespread problem in the tech industry. To make strides toward diversity, we recommend taking a new approach to hiring. Some employees raise concerns about intentionally prioritizing diversity when considering candidates for a given position, assuming that if it plays a role, then the company must be *compromising* on the quality of the hire in some other way. We think this is an incorrect way of looking at it and requires a fundamental reorientation. Instead of asking, "Which person do we think best meets or exceeds the qualifications for this specific role," ask the question, "In filling this role, which person would contribute most to our *collective* ability to achieve outcomes for our customers?"

By reframing the question this way, you may find that the person with an academic background that more closely matches your customers' makes a better hire than the fifth consecutive Ivy League MBA, that the more emotionally attuned individual will challenge the team to think in new ways that yet another analytically minded data geek wouldn't, or that someone who's had very different life circumstances or experiences will be able to find a way to tap into them and broaden the existing team's perspective.

Ben's Story
AN ARMY OF INTJs

While I was at eBay, the product management team grew to over a hundred people. When the company conducted a Myers-Briggs profile assessment, results revealed that *half* of those product managers were INTJs. The INTJ personality type, often called the "Architect" or "Strategist," makes up only 2 percent of the population (and less than 1 percent of women). I was one of those INTJs.

For so many of the product managers to share such a rare personality type meant that there were too many like-minded people in the product team. Because like-minded people tend to hire like-minded people, it was a self-perpetuating problem. I didn't recognize it at the time, but upon reflecting many years later, *I* was part of the problem. I was guilty of allowing a bias toward "Architects" and "Strategists" to shape my feedback on candidates, and I hadn't yet come to appreciate the importance of bringing in a fresh perspective to a team.

Thankfully, once our leadership recognized this overconcentration of a single personality type, it took an active effort to hire more diverse candidates in product management, and I learned a tremendous amount through my interactions with those later hires. I honestly don't think that I would have ever gained an awareness of my own blind spots, nor a desire to address them, without that experience of working with a more diverse peer group.

Ideally, a new hire brings something—experience, personality, or perspective—that no one else on the team currently possesses. Often, people think of "culture fit" as a new hire *matching* with the people on the team or, worse yet, someone that it would be cool to grab a beer with, which is how "bro cultures" form and metastasize. Proper culture fit is actually about *extending* the team's capacity to exhibit the values you aspire to embody.

Rethink Impact, the largest US-based impact fund that invests in female leaders using tech to solve the world's biggest problems, leverages this concept as a core underpinning of its investment thesis. Founder and Managing Partner Jenny Abramson makes clear that, "Diverse teams aren't just good for the world, they're also good business. Studies have shown that the most diverse companies are also the most innovative, have better margins, and have higher revenue. Our venture capital fund, Rethink Impact, was in many ways founded on this notion that inclusive teams help drive optimal outcomes."

Similarly, companies tend to think that every product manager needs to have industry experience in order to provide value to the team. In company after company, we find leaders who are afraid to hire product managers with limited domain expertise. They're convinced that a lack of domain expertise will cause them to fail, but we've seen that hiring someone with *too much* domain expertise carries its own risk. Remember, as a technology company, you want to hire product managers who are going to innovate. If they are steeped in domain expertise, they might be unmotivated or *unable* to think about revolutionary approaches that are needed to deliver a 10x outcome for your customers.

Rajesh's Story

BUILDING SOFTWARE USERS LOVE

After I joined Morningstar, we went through an Agile transformation that focused on user-centricity. Internally, the transition was known as Building Software Users Love. As a part of that transition, I reported directly to the Head of Individual Investor Business (our consumer product suite that included Morningstar.com) rather than the President of Retirement Solutions, whose clients bought the financial wellness/retirement robo-advisor product suite I managed. Why? Because we wanted to introduce a diversity of product perspectives into the group.

Historically, most of the product managers for the robo-advisor platform came from other parts of the retirement business, were familiar with how the industry and clients thought about the product category, and often had a deep technical understanding of the product (and therefore knew its limitations). Since the product was so big and complex, we had a team of a senior product manager (SPM) and three associate product managers (APMs) who rotated frequently as a part of the Morningstar Development Program. When recruiting these APMs, we looked for who could improve the diversity of perspective on the team by bringing a consumer product mindset and questioning why things worked the way they did as we replatformed the product.

As a part of their homework, APMs were asked a simple question about the product (which all of them had access to through Morningstar's own retirement plan): *what one change would you make to the product and why?* The responses quickly identified good design-oriented candidates and the great candidates were able to rationalize why their product change helped both users and the business.

These APMs were mentored by an SPM who also wanted to bring a new mindset to the product team. They were supported by a team of consumer product designers, who collaborated with designers across the organization (especially the Individual Investor Business) to bring a refreshed set of design principles, patterns and best practices. Collectively, these new team members improved the diversity of perspective across the team and led by example to show what it means to be user-centric.

ACTION CHECKLIST AND RESOURCES

Visit *buildwhatmattersbook.com* for an action checklist and resources to help with your product hires, additional information on building and organizing your product teams, and more tips for creating a healthy product-driven culture.

VISION-LED PRODUCT MANAGEMENT

As you finish this book, our hope is that you now understand why having an *end-state vision of the customer experience* is so important to the success of your product and the efficiency of your team, and you have some concrete ideas about how you're going to create your own vision and begin executing it.

That vision becomes your rallying cry, aligning cross-functional teamwork among product, sales, marketing, engineering, and design teams to create a better customer experience by delivering massive value. As you create your vision, we recommend a longer-term horizon, perhaps three years. Even if you're a startup with more urgent fundraising needs, you still need an end-state vision that provides direction to your product development efforts and gives investors context for where you're headed.

Start by creating your customer outcome pyramids so you can measure the success of your product from the customer's perspective *and* your business perspective. Imagine a bold customer experience that would be transformative in delivering that outcome, then map out how a customer journey would yield that 10x outcome. Be sure not to overlook important steps in the customer journey, as it will only be as strong as its weakest link.

Recognize that a vision alone is not enough. You also need a *strategic plan* for making it a reality that takes into account the business constraints and other inevitable pitfalls you will encounter. Get cross-functional agreement to your strategy as a path to realizing the vision, but be willing to change course as needed. Set milestones to keep track of your progress and create natural pivot points to adapt your strategy.

Once you have a vision and strategy, you need to create a *balanced roadmap*. Your individual product managers have to make decisions on a sprint-to-sprint basis, but without a balanced roadmap, it's easy for them to get sidetracked from the vision and strategy as they are nudged toward incremental product improvements that offer only fleeting business benefits.

A balanced roadmap keeps your product managers accountable, connecting their day-to-day decisions about features and sprints to the long-term picture, while simultaneously creating space for the most important product enhancements and operational improvements. That's why we recommend making a decision up-front about the percentage of time that's going into each of the three roadmap categories: innovation, iteration, operation. Tag individual tasks and count them quarterly to make sure your actual allocation matches what you intended. With an awesome end-state vision, an effective strategy, and a balanced roadmap, you need the right *processes*, *people* and *culture* to make it a reality.

Remember the ten product dysfunctions from chapter one? Let's take a look at how Vision-Led Product Management solves each of them:

HOW VISION-LED PRODUCT MANAGEMENT SOLVES THE TOP TEN PRODUCT DYSFUNCTIONS

Dysfunctional Pattern	How Vision-Led Product Management Resolves It
The Hamster Wheel: a focus on output over outcomes	Instead of focusing on simply hitting deadlines, with an output that isn't necessarily meaningful or beneficial, you now have customer outcomes and strategic milestones to measure progress against. Consequently, you know you are creating value for the customer.
The Counting House: an obsession with internal metrics	Instead of obsessing over internal metrics with no regard for customer success, you are now delivering products that customers actually care about.
The Ivory Tower: a lack of customer research	Instead of being so far removed from customers that you risk building products nobody wants or needs, you are now creating solutions based on real market and customer insights.
The Science Lab: optimization to the exclusion of all else	Instead of focusing on superficial improvements to your product driven by A/B tests that produce inconsequential results, you are now taking meaningful strides towards an innovative vision.

Dysfunctional Pattern	How Vision-Led Product Management Resolves It
The Feature Factory: an assembly line of features	Instead of spending most of your time trying to say yes to every customer by adding random features to your product, you are now comfortable selectively saying no and making strategic product investments that propel your company forward.
The Business School: the overuse of science and data	Instead of being paralyzed by intricate analysis and estimation exercises, you can now confidently make strategic decisions that maximize the impact of product development.
The Roller Coaster: fast-paced twists and turns	Instead of making whiplash decisions driven by a lack of immediate results, you can stabilize strategy and have confidence the team is working on the right priorities to deliver value over the long run.
The Bridge to Nowhere: overengineering for future unknowns	Instead of overengineering your product, trying to meet future needs that may never be relevant, you now gain clarity about where infrastructure is truly needed.
The Negotiating Table: trying to keep everyone happy	Instead of trying to give every stakeholder in the company what they want by "horse trading," you now consistently prioritize the product investments for the customer and the company as a whole.
The Throne Room: whipsaw decision-making from the person in charge	Instead of the founder/CEO making decisions about anything and everything in the company, you now have cross-team alignment that is written down and agreed to. Consequently, every initiative can be properly evaluated to determine if it contributes to the end-state customer vision, and the company is primed to scale.

We opened the book by explaining that product management is a paradox. Doing it successfully requires coming up with a single solution that somehow perfectly meets the needs of the dual interests of the customer and the business.

We chose the keystone and arch visual for the book cover intentionally. We imagine the ancients envisioning the ability to "walk through walls" and then building the first arch from a pile of stones. Coupled with repeatability, their innovation changed the world. We see modern product management as a similar undertaking; through ingenuity, conceptualization, planning, adjustments, hard work, and adherence to principles, what once seemed impossible becomes a reality. The arch is a good example of product management at play—a repeatable technology solution that produced a 10x outcome for a broad market.

The arch is also a great metaphor for the Vision-Led Product Management framework itself. A stack of stones on one side represents the customer, and a stack of stones on the other represents the business. *Product management* functions as the *keystone* creating the mutual support that prevents either stack of stones from toppling over as they converge.

Neither a stable arch nor a successful product comes together by accident. They require a vision for the final outcome, a blueprint that the entire team understands and that will define their work. Based on this illustrated vision, a strategic plan gets set. In the case of an arch, it requires collecting stones, carving them to precise shapes, a system for lifting the stones, scaffolding, and so on. Similarly, for a software product, it requires understanding customer needs, identifying market opportunities, building essential technical infrastructure, and layering on the performance features and delighters that will create a complete MVP. Just as arches can be built upon arches to create wonders such as the Colosseum, working code that delivers customer and business value can be layered onto existing products to form the backbone of an enduring business.

Putting Vision-Led Product Management in place may seem like a lot of work, and it won't all happen overnight, but it was true in Lao Tzu's time and it remains true now: "The journey of a thousand miles begins with a single step." We've tried to provide a tangible set of actions at the end of each chapter to help you on your way. Go back and review those actions, share them with your colleagues, and get started as soon as possible to realize the full potential of your product.

To help you put the takeaways from this book directly into action, we'll conclude by providing a summary of the steps to implement Vision-Led Product Management:

OUTLINE FOR IMPLEMENTING VISION-LED PRODUCT MANAGEMENT

We covered a lot of detail on Vision-Led Product Management, but here's a distilled version of what you can do to implement the framework:

1. Assess what your product team is doing well or poorly using the 10 Dysfunctions of Product Management (chapter one).

2. Explain the value of being product-driven and the Vision-Led Product Management framework to

colleagues to gauge interest in exploring this path for the company (chapter two).

3. If the team agrees to use Vision-Led Product Management, the first step is to create customer and business outcome pyramids to define your success metrics (chapter three).

4. Craft a customer journey vision to 10x your key customer outcome using visual artifacts like a comic strip and mock-ups (chapter four).

5. Work backward from that customer journey vision to create a product strategy and strategic milestones everyone can work towards (chapter five).

6. Determine your top-down roadmap allocation and prioritization frameworks across the three categories of product development: innovation, iteration, and operation (chapter six).

7. Establish the processes you need to maintain your outcome pyramids, vision, strategy, and roadmap and to make progress by shipping product changes efficiently (chapter seven).

8. Put the right team in place by carefully considering the people you hire, the org structure you put them in and the culture that surrounds them (chapter eight).

On step three above, we note that it's best to get agreement on using this framework before investing the necessary time to do so. We want you to be successful in your Vision-Led Product Management efforts. While we've created resources at *buildwhatmattersbook.com* to help you get started quickly with all of this, doing so requires a reasonable time commitment from you and, to a lesser extent, your colleagues.

Bringing Vision-Led
Product Management to Your Company

While we did our best to present the concepts and real-world application of Vision-Led Product Management concepts simply in this book, we know making these types of changes isn't easy. If you like what you've read or have tried some of our online resources, we encourage you to connect with us to learn more about who we serve and how we can help. We offer variations of the following core services to founders, CEOs, product executives, product team leads, individual PMs, and investors. Many clients use multiple services and have opted to continue working with us for years as their product needs evolve.

 Strategic Planning: guiding teams to identify their key customer outcome, defining a customer journey vision, and crafting a product strategy to realize that vision

 Training/Speaking: explaining the value of being product-driven and how to use Vision-Led Product Management to help the company achieve its mission

 Coaching: helping individual product people and entire teams deliver more customer and business value, sharpen their product skills, feel more confident in their decisions, get our perspective and advice, and ultimately reach their career goals

 Hiring: validating the need for a product hire, tailoring the job description and homework to the company's needs, screening candidates, and providing a final recommendation on each candidate

 Consulting: serving as an interim product management leader or as an individual product manager, conducting and summarizing user research, and establishing the right product culture and operations

We talk to lots of companies about their product challenges, and we're always glad to meet more to provide some high-level guidance based on their specific situation. So please visit *www.prodify.group* or email us directly at *hello@prodify.group*—we're here to help.

ACKNOWLEDGEMENTS

We wanted to take the time to thank the people who shaped the creation of Vision-Led Product Management and this book, either directly or indirectly:

Our clients who welcomed us into their companies and let us share their product stories with the world:

- Ordergroove—Paul Fredrich
- Storyblocks—TJ Leonard, Michael Sherman, and Ben Sachs
- MarketSmart—Elizabeth Weiland
- DrFirst—Valerie Garrison
- Octopus—Brad Sayler and Cherian Thomas
- Contactually— Tony Cappaert and Zvi Band
- Whoop—Will Ahmed
- CrossLead—Paige Morschauser
- 10% Happier—Derek Haswell and Eva Breitenbach
- WeSpire - Susan Hunt Stevens

The thought leaders who contributed their ideas to this book: Marty Cagan, Christian Idiodi, Melissa Perri, Holly Hester-Reilly, Bruce McCarthy, Dan Olsen, Gibson Biddle, Jenny Abramson, and Eric Paley.

Everyone who endorsed *Build What Matters* or shared it with their colleagues and followers.

The exceptional people who contributed with helpful insights and feedback throughout the process: David Jesse, Sara Zalowitz, Margaret Jastrebski, Herschel Kulkarni, Bruce McCarthy, Jeffrey Rayport, and Melissa Perri.

Jeffrey Miller, whose masterful writing and editing skills helped us share Vision-Led Product Management in simple yet powerful words, and Maggie Rains, who kept us on track.

The managers and mentors who left a lasting impact on Rajesh's product management philosophy and career: Ben Foster, Wayne Lin, Michael Yoch, Steve Wendel, James McClamroch, Tracy Feliciani, and Jody Gustafson (who gave him the chance to transition from software engineer to business analyst and thus kicked off his product career).

Rajesh's family: his wife, Kripa, who spent countless weekends with the kids as he wrote the book; his parents, who nurtured his curiosity, a trait that no doubt got him to where he is today.

Ben's family: his father David, who was also his high school English teacher, for being patient with him when he needed it most; his mother Lori, who instilled the work ethic it demanded; his teenage children Alisha and Rajan, who showed unbelievable understanding and appreciation throughout the process; and most of all to his wife Ami, whose dedication, encouragement, feedback, and support were instrumental.

Made in the USA
Middletown, DE
29 December 2020